SHAKESPEARE AND THE PLAYERS

... *But pardon, gentles all,*
The flat, unraised spirits that have dared
On this unworthy scaffold to bring forth
So great an object: can this cockpit hold
The vasty fields of France? Or may we cram
Within this wooden O the very casques
That did affright the air at Agincourt?

FROM THE PROLOGUE TO Henry V

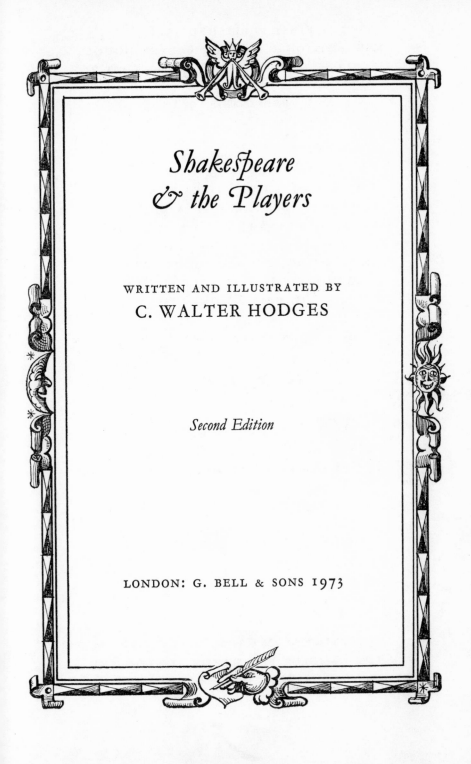

Shakespeare & the Players

WRITTEN AND ILLUSTRATED BY
C. WALTER HODGES

Second Edition

LONDON: G. BELL & SONS 1973

FIRST PUBLISHED 1948
NEW EDITION © 1970 C. WALTER HODGES
PUBLISHED BY G. BELL & SONS LTD, WC2

REPRINTED 1973

ISBN 0 7135 1610 0

PRINTED IN GREAT BRITAIN BY
THE CAMELOT PRESS LTD., LONDON AND
SOUTHAMPTON

For
GRETA

Foreword to the Second Edition

The world of Shakespeare's theatre in the London of Queen Elizabeth and King James I was, and is still, a piece of history unlike any other. There, for the first time, an important part of a nation's cultural life was entirely created not by the wealthy purses of Church or State, or for the private pleasures of great lords, but by common citizens, of the sons of tradesmen from side streets and country towns, working together on their own. It is true that they had some encouragement from great persons in high places; but equally they were opposed by others, not least by the powerful governors of the city they worked in. So in effect, it was by themselves that they created their own style of drama, their own theatre buildings, their own working conditions, and their own public. Their work lasted just about the span of one lifetime, and when they had gone they left behind them a great collection of poems, plays, letters, bills, contracts, jokes, quarrels, songs and music, and a long roll of honour of famous names, headed by Shakespeare's own. And then it was all over. The world of Shakespeare's theatre is like an island in the sea of history, complete in itself; yet every essential part of the life and work of the theatre of all times can be found and studied in it. That, besides its own remarkable story, is that it has always been found so attractive by so many people. The island is magnetic. One is almost drawn to go and live there.

I first became infected with an enthusiasm for this subject many years ago when I was asked to make a single drawing of Shakespeare in his theatre; and so I began to look for details. That one drawing became many, and I began to study all the books I could find, especially Sir Edmund Chambers' four classic volumes of *The Elizabethan Stage*. I was also very much influenced by George R. Kernodle's *From Art to Theatre*, and by John Cranford Adams' *The Globe Playhouse: Its Design and Equipment*. With this latter book and the reconstruction it offered I came in the end to disagree, but I still remember and am greatly indebted to its richly fascinating quality. Also at that time I began to pester people wih letters as king for information, and received much patient help from the antiquarian architect Walter H. Godfrey, and from Professor Allardyce Nicoll who was then director of the Shakespeare Institute at Stratford-on-Avon. I remain very grateful for their criticism and advice.

This little book, then, was the first fruit of my enthusiasm, and it was written chiefly to provide a framework within which to work out some pictures I very much wanted to draw. I have since drawn many others, and in some details, especially as regards the features of the playhouses, I have changed my mind and drawn them rather differently. For ordinary purposes, however, and bearing in mind that in spite of everything that has been written, or perhaps ever will be, there is still no certain knowledge about what Shakespeare's theatre looked like in all its corners, I have been happy to decide that in this new edition, for better or worse, the original pictures may be allowed to stay as they were. I think they give a right impression. I have added a few new ones, made a few slight alterations. Also, I have added a little to the text here and there, and have put in at the end a short collection of extracts from letters and other documents from the theatre-world of that time. Perhaps these may help to explain or justify, or even pass on to others, the infection I have so much enjoyed.

C. W. H.
Bishopstone, 1970

7

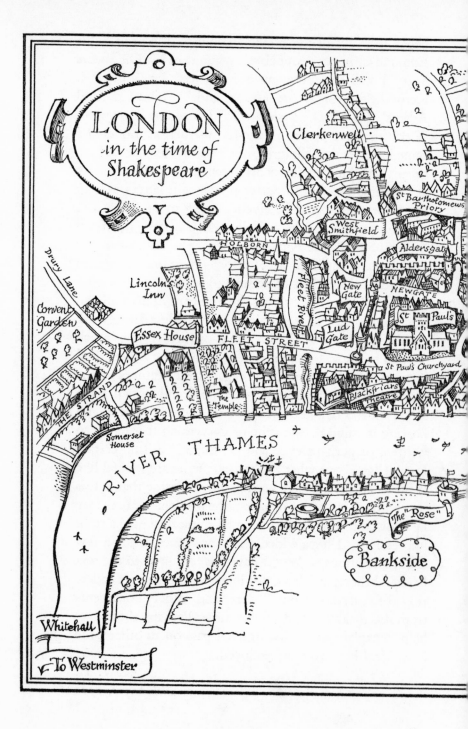

Finsbury Fields

The "Theatre"

The "Curtain"

Shoreditch

Spittle Fields

Moor Fields

Cripplegate

Moorgate

Bishopsgate

BISHOPSGATE STREET

Houndsditch

Guildhall

Aldgate

CHEAPSIDE

e Mermaid Tavern

T CHEAP

GRACIOUS STREET

FENCHURCH St

East Smithfield

Postern Gate

TOWER STREET

een Hythe

St Saviour's

Bellings Gate
LONDON
BRIDGE

THE TOWER

The "Globe"

SOUTHWARK HIGH STREET

Southwark

The distance from St Paul's to the Tower
is one mile: and from Bankside
to Shoreditch is one mile & a half.

Contents

Illustrations

1.   *The Strolling Players*

When William Shakespeare was a boy there was no such thing in all England as a theatre.   Nobody had ever heard of a building specially kept for the performance of plays.   Play-acting, the little there was of it, had always been done on wooden scaffolds in market-places, streets and yards, as part of the celebration of the great festivals of the Christian year.   The plays, usually derived from stories in the Bible, were acted by the townsfolk themselves.   Each of the guilds of a town would have its own scene, and its own little stage: the Skinners' Guild would do the story of Noah, the Grocers' the Judgement of Solomon, the Butchers' Daniel in the Lions' Den, and so on.   But this kind of play-acting was very old even when Shakespeare was young, and was slowly being forgotten.   Instead, the townsfolk of the provincial towns of England, even of small towns like Stratford-on-Avon (where Shakespeare was born in 1564), looked forward to the summer visits of the players from London.

These were professional actors who had formed themselves into companies, each under the patronage of some nobleman whose livery they were entitled to wear. Thus one company would call itself the Earl of Sussex's Men, another Lord Hunsdon's Men, and so on. There was even a company of Queen Elizabeth's Men. Their titles were very high-sounding, but I doubt that to meet a company of players going along the road on a dusty afternoon between one town and the next, you would have thought them much to look at. There would be about nine or ten of them, with a couple of lads who played women's parts (since in those days it was thought disgraceful for real women to appear on the stage), and they travelled, some on foot, some on horseback carrying all their gear in baskets on a donkey, or in a cart. They had playbills printed stating who they were and what pieces they were going to act, and one or two of them would go ahead to paste them up, and make all the arrangements at the next town. They went first to the mayor, and if he thought well of them he would invite them to play at the town hall, and he himself would honour them by being present at their first performance. But at other places, or if there was no suitable hall, they might have to put up their stage in the yard of the inn.

Players were not always welcome among the more respectable people. "Hark, hark, the dogs do bark, the beggars are coming to town: Some in rags and some in tags and some in scarlet gown." Say "players" instead of "beggars" and you have a good idea of how they appeared to many self-respecting people of Shakespeare's day. At least, of his early days.

Their performances were of all kinds: plays, clowning, dancing, juggling, or acrobatic shows; they had to be ready for anything. Their standard of performance was high, and many of their companies were famous not only throughout England, but in places overseas. In Holland, Germany and Denmark there are many old record-books which tell of visits by "The English Comedians".

We know from the records at Stratford that the players were often there. Probably they came regularly once a year. Shakespeare, so far as we know, lived all his boyhood there. His father was a well-to-do tradesman, one of the aldermen of the town, and William went to the Stratford Grammar School. He must often have stopped to watch the players coming down the street, all in their motley clothes, with drum and trumpet before them, like one of those travelling circus parades that may still be seen—though they are becoming rare—in remote country towns, even today; and if so we may be sure he would follow behind them with the other boys, and push his way into the Guildhall to see the show.

2. The Queen at Kenilworth

When Shakespeare was eleven years old Queen Elizabeth came in state to Kenilworth, where she stayed for three weeks at the castle as guest of the great Earl of Leicester. All her courtiers came with her, with all their servants and men-at-arms. The occasion, known since then as the Princely Pleasures of Kenilworth, is remembered as having been the most splendid display of pageantry in her reign—a reign famous for pageantry. Day after day there were hunting and feasting, plays and masques and dances, the shooting off of cannon by day and fireworks by night, with everywhere music and fine dresses. Kenilworth is only a walking distance from Stratford and it would be very surprising if young Will Shakespeare had not gone there with his family, among the crowds from all the near-by places, to see something of the spectacle; and perhaps he may have had a glimpse of some of the theatrical displays which were given in the Queen's honour on the lawns before the castle.

Such displays, though they were not often on so large a scale, were not uncommon; indeed Queen Elizabeth,

like all great sovereigns of her time, whenever she travelled in state through the country, would expect to be received with ceremonial pageantry at every important town she came to. Much money and skill were spent upon the presentation of these shows, which usually took the form of recitals of music and poetry given by people dressed as characters from British or classical mythology, such as Queen Mab or Hercules; or somebody dressed as the founder or patron saint of the town would come to welcome the Queen within the gates. All this would be done with lavish decoration on ornamental stages, or with triumphal arches surmounted by figures in pageant dress, scattering flowers and perfumes on the Queen as she passed by. Or the show might be

given on the waters of a lake. This was a favourite device. At Kenilworth there was a water display in which the Lady of the Lake was carried off by Orion riding on a dolphin. At another entertainment given for the Queen by the Earl of Hertford some years later, the Earl had had prepared a whole artificial lake, complete with three "islands" in it. One was built up to represent a ship, full of cannon to fire salutes for the

Queen; one a fort; and one a hill shaped rather like a snail shell, and so called a "Snail Mount". Upon the lake there floated a little pinnace, with a nymph and her maidens in it singing, and this was pulled along to the shore, where the Queen awaited it, by a group of people representing Neptune and his attendant Tritons, dressed "with grisly heads and beards of divers colours and fashions". This is the scene which I show in the picture on pages 16 and 17.

The actors in these performances were usually ladies and gentlemen of the Court; but professional players were often employed as well, probably for the longer speaking parts where trained voices were required. The Earl of Leicester had his own company of players, which would certainly have been at Kenilworth during the Queen's visit. This company was led by a certain James Burbage, who may rightly be said to be one of the founders of the English theatre as we know it today, because in the year following his return to London after the Princely Pleasures of Kenilworth, he opened the first public theatre ever built in England.

3. The First "Plaie Howses"

As the summer drew to an end most of the players' companies came back from the country to winter quarters in London, where they performed throughout the winter. Before James Burbage built his theatre the best places for these performances, in London as in the country, had been in the open yards of the great inns. If you will look at the map of old London on pages 8 and 9 you will see Gracious Street (it is called Gracechurch Street today), which was a part of the great main road going north and south through the City. It was here, and along the main streets crossing it, that the principal inns were found, and here, when the plays were on, all the street outside would be crowded with folk going in. They were not always the best kind of people either. All the commotion, the blocking of the streets and the quarrelling, to say nothing of the hucksters and beggars it brought together, were naturally looked on with great dislike by the City authorities and the more respectable folk; and, as the plays were so often given on Sundays and on religious feast-days, they were especially disliked by those religiously-minded people who were then beginning to be known as Puritans. Plays, said the Puritans, were "the nest of the Divel and the sink of all sin. . . . They are public enemies to virtue and religion; . . . and bring both the Gospel into slander; the Sabbath into contempt; men's souls into danger; and finally the whole Commonweal into disorder." The Lord Mayor wrote to the Privy Council complaining that the plays caused "unthrifty waste of money by poor persons, sundry robberies by picking and cutting of purses, uttering of seditious matters, and many other corruptions of youth, and other enormities; besides also sundry slaughters and maimings of the Queen's subjects, that have happened by falling scaffolds, frames, and stages, and by engines, weapons and powder used in plays". But for all these complaints, and many others like them that were uttered from almost every pulpit in London, year in year out, the plays became increasingly popular, and larger and larger crowds gathered to see them. New plays, new poets, new actors had to be found to cope with the growing demand for this new field of entertainment which was rising almost out of nothing, just as in recent times television has grown up and become a part of everybody's life.

However, whatever else you may have thought about the rights and wrongs of going to the play in those days,

there was one good reason for staying away which nobody could deny. Queen Elizabeth's London was never
quite free of the plague. It came nearly every summer,
and of course where there were big sweating crowds of
people who didn't wash very often—and that, quite
plainly, is what most of the people were like—the infection spread rapidly among them. In those days
nobody knew what caused the disease; but since it so
often seemed to start among the crowds at the play,
respectable people used to think it came as a judgement
from God upon the sinful places where play performances were held. In any event it was wisely decreed by
the City Council that whenever the plague appeared in
London all performances of plays should cease, and when
this happened the players packed up and took themselves
off into the country again.

From among the great many letters and other documents about the London theatre-world of this time that
have been handed down to us, a few extracts have been
collected together in a little anthology at the end of this
book. Here, on page 95, you may read a letter from the
City Council refusing to allow the players to gather
crowds together, even when the plague had subsided to
what was claimed to be a "safe" level. Another docu-
ment shows how attempts were made to deprive the
players of the support they had from their powerful friends
and patrons at the Queen's court. This you may read on
page 93.

But try as hard and as often as they might, and though
they nearly succeeded more than once, the Lord Mayor
and his Council never finally succeeded in getting rid of
the players altogether. Doing what they could, however, they at last managed to hedge the players around
with so many local regulations and restrictions, and
generally made life so difficult for them in the City, that
in the end most of the players' companies found it more

worth while to stay in the suburbs, where the City Council had less control.

That was the situation which existed when James Burbage returned from Kenilworth, and he decided that although it was a bad thing to be away from the easy crowds in the centre of town, he might none the less turn the situation to advantage. Away from the narrow streets he would have room to build a "plaie howse" of his own, capable not only of showing his plays at their best, but also of holding much larger audiences than could be crowded into an inn. He borrowed some money and rented a piece of ground in Shoreditch, which in those days was at the end of a grassy little country road—today's Bishopsgate Street—where people used to go on holiday afternoons to watch the archery practice in Finsbury Fields or the Tower gunners firing off cannon in a place called the Artillery Garden. He rented his bit of ground for twenty-one years only. We shall have reason to remember that in a later page.

He built his "plaie howse" of timber. It had three open galleries, one above the other, surrounding a circular yard or arena—an idea Burbage probably copied from the bear-baiting arenas on Bankside, the district on the south bank of the Thames. (Perhaps he reckoned that if the craze for plays fell off he could still use his arena for bear-baiting and suchlike things, instead.) Built out from one side of the yard into the middle was the stage, just a high bare platform. The surrounding galleries were roofed with thatch, but the arena, and probably the stage also, at least in the beginning, was open to the sky. Burbage called this experimental playhouse of his "The Theatre" (being short for "Amphitheatre"). He opened it in 1576.

His venture was such an immediate success that it must have surprised even Burbage himself, and in the following year he built another playhouse, right next door. This, too, prospered. It was called "The Curtain", because it was built on a piece of land called Curtain Field; and there is a street called Curtain Road over the site of it to this day. Shortly afterwards a rival company, run by a certain Philip Henslowe, opened a third playhouse called "The Rose", over on Bankside.

These were the principal theatres that Shakespeare knew when he first came to London.

4.   *Shakespeare comes to London*

Nobody knows for certain when Shakespeare first came to London, though it is generally believed it was in the late fifteen-eighties; perhaps in the year of the Armada, when he was twenty-four. Neither do we know why he left Stratford. There are a number of stories, among which is a favourite one telling how Shakespeare, an unruly young man, was caught poaching deer in Charlecote Park, the home of the local squire Sir Thomas Lucy, and that he fled from Stratford to escape the consequences. Something of the kind may have happened, and it may have led him, as some people think, to join a troupe of players who were passing through Stratford, and go with them overseas to the Low Countries: some say he even went as far as Italy. It is not at all unlikely, and there is much in his writing which seems to show he was very familiar with foreign places. But the most famous story of all is that, arriving in London poor and unknown, he took a job as a horse-boy outside the Theatre, minding the horses of well-to-do patrons while they were in at the play; and that he proved himself so ready and reliable at this job that people soon did not care to entrust their horses to anyone else, and Shakespeare had to employ a number of boys to help him, who used to run

up to patrons as they arrived, calling "I am Shakespeare's boy, sir". Whether this is true or not, it is probable that Shakespeare started his theatrical life in a very modest way, sometimes acting, sometimes giving a helping hand backstage and copying out parts for the other players. And it is likely that he spent some time adapting and rewriting other people's old plays, before his own original genius began to be recognised. It should not be forgotten that although Shakespeare is the supreme poet of the English language he himself never lost sight of the fact that he was an actor writing for actors. He lived all his working life in the theatre as actor, writer and part-owner, and what he didn't know about the theatre, as a workaday job, wasn't worth knowing. But his theatre was so different from the sort of theatre with which we are familiar today that we shall do well to pause here, to look inside and see what sort of a place it was.

5. A Day at the Playhouse

In Queen Elizabeth's time the day started early. People were up and about by four o'clock: children were at school by six.

In the Theatre at Shoreditch, just when the early grey light was beginning, you might have heard a yawn from the place at the back where the actors dressed, and seen a man come sleepily out on to the stage to look at the new day. It was drizzling; there were puddles in the yard. The man looked up at the flagstaff which stood over the top of the house. Here every morning when the weather was fine he hoisted the house flag, which was the sign that a performance would take place that afternoon as usual, beginning at two o'clock. Today he wouldn't hoist the flag just yet.

The man was one of the playhouse servants. He did duty as caretaker, stage-hand, and bill-poster, took walking-on parts in the afternoons, and did odd jobs generally. He went now and unbolted one of the doors in the yard and, seeing two or three of his friends already coming up the path to work, he went out to the ale-house next door to get some beer for his breakfast.

When he came back it was broad daylight, though still drizzly and grey. The stage-keeper had arrived, an oldish man who had been all his life with the players, and was now responsible for everything that went on backstage, just as a stage-manager is today. The man asked him, should he hoist the flag? The stage-keeper scratched his chin. Not yet, he said, leave it a little till Master Burbage came. He would be here shortly for this morning's rehearsal. Meanwhile take a broom and get on with sweeping out the top gallery.

James Burbage, who lived near by, arrived early at the Theatre with his son Richard (who in a few years' time was to become one of the two most famous players of his generation); and soon the whole company was with them, ready to start the day's work. The slow rain showed no sign of stopping. On any ordinary day, unless the rain were very bad, they would hoist the flag and risk it, but today was to be a special day, the first performance of a new play, when, according to custom, all entrance money would be doubled. Would people come in this weather? Would it not be better to wait till tomorrow? Meanwhile the author had arrived and tethered his horse to a railing in the yard. He had just ridden out from the City hoping for the best, and now he stood with the others looking up into the wet sky. He thought he could see a bit of blue.

The author I have in mind for this one day at the

Theatre is Thomas Kyd, and his play is *The Spanish Tragedy*, which was first performed in 1589. After this it soon became so popular that it ran, on and off, for fifty years. (Plays were not then performed for more than a few days at a time, but successful ones were repeated at intervals.) *The Spanish Tragedy*, a dark and baleful play full of ghosts, murders and revenges, was one of the great successes of the stage when Shakespeare first came to town, and he wrote his own *Titus Andronicus* in imitation of its bloodthirsty manner. That, too, was a success. But for the day we are now imagining Shakespeare was not yet on the scene, except as a small-part actor at the morning's rehearsal.

As the morning went on the sky began to brighten. The puddles in the yard began to shine, and only occasional drops of rain fell into them. Without waiting to be told, somebody went and hoisted the flag. Others went off to paste up playbills in Gracious Street and Cheapside, by the main conduits where people drew water, and on the pillars in Paul's Walk, the nave of the Cathedral, which in those days was often more like a market-place than a church, and was where gentlemen of leisure went to walk and talk and show off their best clothes before dinner.

Dinner was at twelve o'clock. The gentlemen in the town went to their eating-houses and talked about the afternoon's new play. At the Theatre the rehearsal was over, and the stage was being strewn with fresh rushes. Outside the entrance the side-shows were being set up: skittle alleys and tobacco booths, jugglers, quack doctors, fortune-tellers, apple-women, horse-boys, and a whole menagerie of rogues and beggars (such as Dommerers, who pretended to be dumb; Abraham-men, who pretended to be mad—"you see pinnes stuck in sundry places of their naked flesh, especially in their armes, only to make you beleeve they are out of their wits"; and

Priggers of Prancers—"To *Prig* signifies in their language to steale, and *Prancer* signifies a horse." They have been described for us in much detail by writers of the time. A brief account by one of them is given here on pages 96–97.)

The day had turned out fine after all, and there was a big crowd by the time the door was opened. Each person passing through put his coin into the box held there by a "gatherer". This first payment only allowed him to go in and stand in the yard among the "groundlings", but once there he could if he chose pay more money at a further entrance which led up from the yard to the galleries, and for seats in the best parts of the galleries there were further payments still. "A penny" is mentioned as the normal unit of payment, but it is difficult to estimate what this would mean in present-day values—probably something well over a shilling; let us say about eight pence in the new English coinage. The most expensive parts of the house were the "Lords' Rooms" and "Gentlemen's Rooms", which were next to the stage, rather like the boxes in a modern theatre. As time went on, and more and more fashionable people began to go to the plays, there was not enough room in the boxes to take them all, and gentlemen began to sit out on the stage in front of them, on stools; and this custom eventually became so popular with the gallants and dandies, and at times there was such a crowd of them smoking and playing cards among themselves in everybody's view whenever they lost interest in the play, or loudly criticising the actors whenever they felt inclined, that in the end they became a thorough nuisance.

But on the day of this first performance of *The Spanish Tragedy* things had not got to that pitch. There would be nobody sitting on the stage. A few fine gentlemen, well-known patrons of the Theatre, were behind the stage watching the players getting into their costumes, or talking with the author and Master Burbage. The Lords' Rooms were already taken up. The better galleries were full and the rest were filling. Sellers of nuts and apples were doing a good trade, and the boys from the ale-house were going in and out with trays of pot ale. Somewhere there might be a cutpurse waiting his chance; somewhere else there might be a couple of quiet men whom Master Henslowe, of the rival company at the Rose, had sent along to write down as much of the play as they could get, in shorthand. They would come several times till they had it all pat, and then Master Henslowe would be able to put on his own pirated version of the play. All players' companies had to guard their plays jealously and keep an eye open for this sort of thing, which was not uncommon.

A trumpet now sounded from the top of the house. It was the first of three soundings, and warned the latecomers in the road to hurry; the second sounding was a signal that the players were ready; and at the third the play would begin.

During the play most of the audience listened closely. Nowadays we go as much to *see* a play as to hear it, but in Shakespeare's time it was the *hearing* that was the thing. Not, as I shall show later, that there was nothing to see; indeed there was much; but the Elizabethans, who were not so used to learning through their eyes, by reading and seeing pictures, as we are today, were above all things a people who liked to stay and listen. They liked hearing music and poetry, they liked listening to witty talk: they would stand for an hour or more listening to a good sermon, and for as long as you liked at a good play. This afternoon they listened with enthusiasm to *The Spanish Tragedy*. They applauded the good actors and "mewed" (so we are told) at the bad ones, but otherwise were rather more quiet than usual. The only disturbance was when the cutpurse was caught red-

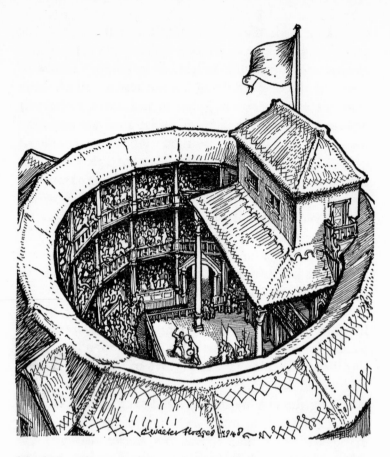

handed. He was taken and tied up to one of the posts on the stage, and in the intervals between the acts he was used as an aiming mark for apple-cores.

The play at last drew to a close; the trumpets sounded a slow march; the "bodies" were carried off; the haggard ghost of Revenge promised to pursue the villains of the piece down—

> "to deepest hell
> Where none but Furies, bugs, and tortures dwell"—

and thereupon disappeared through a trap-door in the floor of the stage. The audience roared approval and then settled down for the last part of the show; for these afternoons were always rounded off with a sort of farcical performance known as a "jig", which was a piece for the clowns and Merry Andrews, made up of puns and back-chat, topical burlesque and lively dancing. The better class of patrons did not stay for it; and, along with these, Master Henslowe's two quiet men slipped out and went home to copy out their notes.

When all was over, and as the doors were being closed on the last of the departing audience, it started to rain again. Old James Burbage, pleased with himself for having been so lucky, retired to his counting-house to reckon up the takings. The total had to be shared out, about half of it going to his partner, who owned what was called the "housekeeping" share of the business, and who kept the building in repair and paid the gatherers and other house servants; and the remainder coming to himself, for him to share again with his actors and stage-keepers, to buy stage equipment and pay the author. By the time he and his partner had worked it all out, the evening was growing dark. Most of the players had gone; the stage-keepers had tidied away today's gear and had got out the new stuff for the morrow. Master Shakespeare brought James Burbage the key of the chest where the playbooks were safely locked away, and went off to supper in London with Thomas Kyd and his friends. Richard Burbage had gone on ahead with some of the musicians. Old James, who had had enough of boisterous evenings in his younger days, now preferred to sup at home with his wife. On his way out of the Theatre he looked up and saw that they had left the flag still flying in the rain. He called out to have it hauled down, and when he had seen it done made his way home alone through the gathering dark.

Presently the caretaker, who had been at supper in the ale-house, came in and locked the door. He retired, yawning, behind the curtains at the back of the stage, and lit a candle to make his bed. When that was done

he blew the candle out, and was soon asleep. In Queen
Elizabeth's time they went to bed early and saved
candles.

6. The Upstart Crow

When Shakespeare first arrived in London the art of
writing plays was, as we have seen, still new, and it was to
be left for Shakespeare himself to show the world what
could be done with it. Still, there were already a
number of clever experimental writers from whom he
learned much of his craft. Plays in those days were often
written by two or three authors working together, and
it is often not possible to tell who wrote which section
of any particular play. For instance, included among
Shakespeare's earliest works are the three parts of the
historical play *Henry VI*. It is not known how much of
this he actually wrote himself, but it is believed that parts
of it are in fact the work of other men. Thomas Kyd
may have had a hand in it, and so may George Peele and
Robert Greene, both famous poets in their time.

George Peele was known more for his colourful
bohemian life than for his plays. We hear of him at one
time as the friend of wealthy City merchants, and as the
creator of pageants for the Lord Mayor's Show; at
another, as a penniless actor unable to pay his rent, and
unable to leave the house (because his landlady had
pawned all his clothes) until in a corner of the cellar he
found an old rusty suit of armour, in which he made his
escape, to the great amusement of the people in the street.
Then we hear of him in an escapade near Oxford where
he was travelling with a troupe of players. Fascinated
by a pretty girl whose father was supposed to be an
invalid, he contrived to get into their house disguised as a
doctor. Just for the fun of the thing, he mixed up for

the old man a horrible brew concocted of all the vilest things he could lay his hands on at random, and having got his "patient" to swallow it, he went away, with the expectation of never seeing him again.   But on his way home some days later he was discovered and reluctantly obliged to go back to the house, to view, as he thought, the corpse of his victim.   But far from it: the old man was not only alive and kicking: he had never been so well for years, and wanted only to reward the "learned doctor" with a sumptuous dinner, in return for his miraculous cure!

These stories, with others of the kind, appeared in a book called *The Merrie Jests of George Peele,* which was published a few years after his death.   They are most unlikely to be true; they are more like the plots of "jigs" and farces than incidents in real life, but they do show the sort of reputation Peele left behind him.   Perhaps, therefore, it is surprising to know that he also left a number of plays containing some poetry of quite unusual charm.   One of his poems is given here on page 98.

A more considerable man was Robert Greene.   He was one of the typical poor scholars of that age, who having worked his way through the University found himself still poor in a world which offered him nothing but the chance to live by his wits.   So he lived a dissolute life, half in and half out of the gutter, with a bully named Cutting Ball, a street gangster, for his companion.   He earned his living by writing plays, books, pamphlets, novels, anything he could sell, and indeed became one of the most popular authors of the time; but of all his work his fame now rests chiefly on a few sentences he wrote shortly before he died.   They are about William Shake-speare, and are indeed the first mention made of him by anyone at all since his arrival in London.   Strangely enough, Greene has not a friendly word to say for him. Instead he calls him an "upstart crow", describes him as having a "tiger's heart wrapped in a player's hide", and warns his fellow-writers to beware of him as one who would steal their work and take their credit for his own. "He supposes," wrote Greene, "that he is as well able to bombast out a blank verse with the best of you; and being an absolute *Johannes factotum,* is in his own conceit the only *Shake-scene* in a country." This attack was published in 1592 in a pamphlet sometimes called *Greene's Repentance,* which he wrote in the last stages of poverty and disease, dying all alone in a slum room over a cobbler's shop. It was the sneer of a jealous and disappointed man who saw how Shakespeare's reputation was rising where his own had fallen away. There is a story that soon after, when Greene lay dead, the cobbler's wife crept up to his room and put a wreath of bay on his head. She was the only person who remembered what a famous poet he once had been.

But most famous of all the poet-dramatists before Shakespeare was Christopher Marlowe. Better than anyone before, he found a way to choose and combine words so that they had an effect of enchantment in which he carried his audience away in their imaginations to share the life of a kind of tapestry-world which he created for them on the stage, full of extreme and violent romance. His greatest plays, *Tamburlaine, Doctor Faustus,* and *The History of Edward II,* are among the finest things in English. Had Marlowe lived longer he might have rivalled Shakespeare himself; but his life, like Greene's, was spent in unsettled times and unruly company. While he was the friend of Sir Walter Raleigh and his circle on the one hand, he mixed with spies and jailbirds on the other. When he was only twenty-nine he was mysteriously stabbed to death in a brawl in the back room of a tavern in Deptford. This happened in 1593, the year after Greene had died, and with it Shakespeare suddenly found himself for the time being without any rival at all.

7. Shakespeare's Progress

The thing that had made Robert Greene so bitterly jealous, and the thing that is so difficult to explain, is that Shakespeare had talent of a kind which is beyond all common explanation, and to which we give the name "genius". Greene and his friends prided themselves on their scholarly training, their University degrees and so on. Shakespeare had none; he was not considered to be an "educated" man in the formal sense. Yet he was born with a skill the others did not have, and when he took up his pen his skill produced itself with the ease of second nature. His friends reported in admiration that "in his writing, (whatsoever he penned) he never blotted out line".

Among his earliest plays are *The Taming of the Shrew*, *Love's Labour's Lost*, and *Richard III*, and we find even by this time that Shakespeare, the player from the Theatre, was also quite at home with the cultured life of Queen Elizabeth's Court. Then, in the year Marlowe was killed, there began a dreadful outbreak of the plague in London, which lasted for nearly two years. The playhouses were closed and the players scattered. Shakespeare at this time wrote and published his two narrative poems, *Venus and Adonis* and *Lucrece*, both of which he dedicated to the young Earl of Southampton, who now became his friend and patron.

When the playhouses opened their doors again, in 1594, Shakespeare was ready with *Romeo and Juliet*, and with that play his great successes began. There followed *A Midsummer Night's Dream*, *Richard II*, *The Merchant of Venice* and the two parts of *Henry IV*, at which it is said Queen Elizabeth laughed so much at the character of the fat Sir John Falstaff that she asked Shakespeare to write another play showing Sir John in love; and it was to fulfil this personal request of the Queen's that Shakespeare wrote *The Merry Wives of Windsor*.

Shakespeare's success was due not only to his genius, but to his good fortune in entering the stage world at a time when, as we have seen, it was rapidly growing in influence and popularity, as no form of entertainment had ever done before. Besides this (and in spite of Greene's bitter remarks), Shakespeare was a very popular, likeable man. He also appears to have been a good business man, for before many years were out he had become one of the principal partners, together with Richard Burbage, in the company which owned and managed the Theatre. He began to grow rich.

8. *Top of the Bill*

It is now time to say something of the famous actors of that day, especially of Richard Burbage, star of his father's company at the Theatre; and of Edward Alleyn, star of the rival company at the Rose.

We first hear of Richard Burbage in the course of a lawsuit (one of many) involving the management of the Theatre. Some men had gone there with a court order to collect a debt. Old James Burbage had shut the door in their faces, and he and his wife were both leaning out of an upper window, shouting abuses at them and bidding them clear off, when in the middle of it all Richard appeared on the scene and set about the wretched men with a broomstick. According to one witness, who tried to intervene on their behalf, "the said Richard Burbage, scornfully and disdainfully playing with this witness's nose, said he would beat him also, and did challenge the

field of him at that time". This appears to have been a
typical Burbage family scene. There was a shindy rather
like it which, as we shall see, contributed to the building
of the Globe; and old James Burbage had long been
known to the City authorities as "a stubborn fellow"
(see page 92). His son Richard soon became a close
friend of Shakespeare, and is thought to have been the
creator of many, if not all, of his great tragic heroes—
Hamlet, King Lear, Macbeth and Othello. He was
especially famous for his performance as Richard III.

In the picture above I show him wearing the

Elizabethan version of a "Roman" costume in the name part of Shakespeare's *Titus Andronicus*. The dress is interesting because it is derived from a drawing, the only one of its kind believed to be in existence, made by someone who actually saw the play on an Elizabethan stage.

Richard Burbage died in 1619, and ended his famous life with a famously appropriate epitaph. It was simply: "Exit Burbage."

His great rival, Edward Alleyn, was especially noted for his performance in the plays of Christopher Marlowe: as Tamburlaine, Doctor Faustus and Barabbas, the Jew of Malta. The picture opposite shows him in the part of Tamburlaine, and the particular incident is in the second part of the play, at Act IV, Scene III, which opens as follows:

Enter TAMBURLAINE, *drawn in his chariot by the* KINGS OF TREBIZON AND SORIA, *with bits in their mouths, reins in his left hand, and in his right hand a whip with which he scourgeth them.* . . .

TAMB.   *Holla, ye pamper'd jades of Asia,*
What, can ye draw but twenty miles a day,
And have so proud a chariot at your heels
And such a coachman as great Tamburlaine . . .

The dress he wears is the Elizabethan version of an "oriental" costume.

Being of Henslowe's Company, Alleyn did not have the chance to work with Shakespeare, and much he may have regretted it. If so, it can have been his only regret. Hand in glove with Henslowe, whose stepdaughter Joan he married, he came to inherit Henslowe's prosperous business, and retired early from the stage, a wealthy man. He then founded the College of God's Gift at Dulwich, whose boys ever since have called themselves "Alleynians". Together with his college he left for posterity a collection of papers, diaries and account-books once belonging to Henslowe and himself, which are now the most valuable record we have of the stage life of his time. Among them are some letters he wrote to his wife while he was away in the country with his company, then called Lord Strange's Men. They give so vivid a picture of his life that it does not come amiss to quote one here. It was written from Bristol in 1593, the year of the terrible plague in London:

My Good Sweet Mouse,

I commend me heartily to you and to my father, my mother, and my sister Bess, hoping in God though the sickness be round about you yet, by His mercy, it may escape your house, which, by the grace of God, it shall. Therefore use this course: keep your house fair and clean, which I know you will, and every evening throw water before your door, and in your back side, and have in your windows good store of rue and herb of grace, and with all the grace of God, which must be obtained by prayers; and so doing, no doubt but the Lord will mercifully defend you.

Now, good mouse, I have no news to send you but this, that we have all our health, for which the Lord be praised. I received your letter at Bristow, by Richard Cowley, for which I thank you.

I have sent you by this bearer, Thomas Pope's kinsman, my white waistcoat, because it is a trouble to me to carry it. Receive it with this letter, and lay it up for me till I come.

If you send any more letters, send to me by the carriers of Shrewsbury or to West Chester or to York, to be kept till my Lord Strange's players come.

And thus, sweetheart, with my hearty commendations to all our friends, I cease from Bristow this Wednesday after St. James his day, being ready to begin the play of *Harry of Cornwall*.

Mouse, do my hearty commends to Mr Grig's wife and all his household, and to my sister Philips.

Your loving husband,

E. Alleyn.

The two greatest comic actors of the period were
Richard Tarlton and Will Kempe.   Tarlton, it is true,
was a little before Shakespeare's day (he died in 1588)
but he was so well remembered throughout Shakespeare's lifetime that he has a right to be mentioned here.
He is said to have been the original of the jester Yorick,
whom Hamlet speaks of in the play.   He was the Queen's
favourite clown.   A memory of him, published in later
years, is that "when Queen Elizabeth was *serious* (I dare
not say *sullen*) and out of *good humour*, he could *un-dumpish*
her at his pleasure".   He was at one time the leader of a
company called "The Queen's Men", for whom he
wrote plays and jigs, and there is a story of them in the
country, and of a pompous local Justice who came to see

their show: "They were now entering into their first merriment (as they call it), and the people began exceedingly to laugh when Tarlton first peeped out his head. Whereat the Justice, not a little moved, and seeing with his becks and nods he could not make them cease, he went with his staff and beat them on the bare pates, in that

Will Kempe

they, being but farmers and poor country hinds, would presume to laugh at the Queen's men, and make no more account of her cloth in his presence."

Tarlton's portrait on page 41, which I have adapted from a woodcut on the cover of a book called *Tarlton's Jests* (*Full of Delight, Wit, and Honest Mirth*), shows him stepping a dance to the accompaniment of his own pipe and tabor. Clowning and dancing went together. This was especially so in the case of the famous clown Will

Kempe. As a dancer he held (and probably still holds) the world's long-distance record, for in 1597 he laid a wager he would dance a morris from London to Norwich: which he did. It took him nine days, and his going was something like a triumph. All the way along when they heard he was coming, people flocked to see him pass, and when he reached Norwich he had hardly room to dance through the crowd. He was welcomed by the Mayor and Guilds of the City, who gave him a life pension, made him a freeman of their city, and nailed up his dancing shoes in the Guildhall in memory of the great occasion. He afterwards wrote the full story of the exploit in a little book, *Kempe's Nine Days Wonder*, from the cover of which I have taken his portrait. It shows him with his piper, Thomas Sly.

On the stage he acted with the Burbage company. He is known to have played in Shakespeare's *Romeo and Juliet* and *Much Ado About Nothing*, in which he created the part of Constable Dogberry. He must also have been one of the clowns in *A Midsummer Night's Dream*: did he perhaps play Bottom the Weaver?

9. The Boy Players

As has been pointed out earlier, women never appeared on the stage in Shakespeare's day, and women's parts were always played by boys. They were apprenticed when they were about ten years old to individual actors, who were responsible for training them and paying them their wages; and they remained apprentices until they were fifteen or sixteen. They were required to have good voices, a talent for acting, and if possible some talent for music as well. They had frequently to sing and play the lute. It will be noted that there are usually not many women's parts in the action of an Elizabethan play, but the few there are often demand a high degree of skill. Juliet and Lady Macbeth, for example, are not parts for actors of poor quality, and Shakespeare, writing for players whose individual abilities he knew well, would never have written such parts had he not been sure that they would be rendered in a way to do them justice.

It is interesting to recall, by the way, the use Shakespeare makes of the device of dressing up his heroines in boys' clothes, as for example in *Twelfth Night* and *As You Like It*: a simple but clever way of turning the condition to advantage.

But as well as the boy apprentices in the men's companies there were for a time two famous companies composed entirely of boys. These were "The Children of Paul's" and "The Children of the Chapel Royal". Originally they had been recruited solely as choirboys, but being under Royal patronage they were sometimes used to give recitals at Court entertainments, and having well-trained voices and a pretty way of speaking verse, their choirmasters put them to learning and reciting plays. It may be imagined that the boys entered into the spirit of the thing with a will, and their performances soon became so fashionable that for a while they became serious rivals to the men's companies in the public playhouses. The children did not play in public, but in so-called "private" playhouses, where the conditions were very different. They had covered halls, they performed in the evening by candlelight, and they admitted only the better sort of audience, not the groundling riff-raff of the open houses. Their theatres were in the City itself: the Children of the Chapel Royal at Blackfriars; the Children of Paul's, as their name implies, in a building by the Cathedral.

Of course, we must suppose that these boys were

mostly willing members of their companies, but their acting abilities were for a time so profitable to their masters that those gentlemen began to make very free use of the special authority they had to enlist boys as "choristers" in the Royal Chapels. In one case they actually kidnapped a boy on his way home from school, and his father had to take the matter to the Privy Council before he could get him released. And a famous actor of later years, one Nathan Field, was said to have been started on his career, when a boy, in just such a way as this.

The plays written for the boys' companies were no different from those of any other company. There was not the slightest attempt to make them "fit for children". On the contrary, there was a time when they specialised in the most horrific kinds of blood-and-thunder plays which, from their being acted almost in darkness, save for the light of one or two eerie candles, came to be known as "nocturnals".

Of their comedies, *The Knight of the Burning Pestle,* by Beaumont and Fletcher, is still a favourite, but it is not always realised that this play was written to be acted entirely by children. The opening scene of this play, which gives an amusing picture of what stage conditions were sometimes like in those days, with the Grocer and his wife climbing up on to the stage and arguing with the actors, is given here on pages 105–10. You will notice that the Grocer addresses the actor as "goodman boy".

10. *The End of the "Theatre"*

You will remember that old James Burbage had built the Theatre on a plot of ground for which he had a lease of only twenty-one years. In the twenty-first year he died, leaving the Theatre to his two sons, Richard and

Cuthbert. Since their tenancy of the ground on which it was built was then on the point of running out, this bequest was of doubtful value. The brothers sent to the landlord, asking him to renew the lease. The landlord did not reply. It must be admitted that the Burbage family were not the best of tenants; their twenty-one years had been notable for brawls and riots. The landlord would have been glad to be rid of them; and besides, he reckoned the Burbages, when their lease expired, would have to leave the Theatre, with the ground it stood on, to him. There was a fortune in it. So when they sent to him he simply did not answer.

To this the Burbage brothers, with Shakespeare and their other partners, guessing what was in the wind, had a ready answer. They rented another plot of ground over on Bankside; they engaged a builder—Peter Street, his name was—who just after Christmas in the year 1598 began to pull down the Theatre and to cart its timbers over the river for rebuilding on the new site.

As soon as he heard of this, the landlord tried hard to have it stopped. He claimed that Street, the builder, was trespassing on his ground, and sent some men to prevent him carting the stuff away; whereupon, as he complained to the magistrates afterwards, the Burbage party "then and there armed themselves with diverse and many unlawful and offensive weapons, as namely swords, daggers, bills, axes and such like, and so armed did then repair unto the said Theatre, and then and there armed as aforesaid, in very riotous, outrageous and forcible manner . . . attempted to pull down the said Theatre". His own people, he said, were "going about in peaceable manner to procure them to desist from that unlawful enterprise". But in vain: the Burbage party resisted strongly, "pulling, breaking and throwing down the said Theatre in very outrageous, violent and riotous sort".

At least they did not throw it down so violently that it could not be rebuilt. From the timbers of the old Theatre a fine new playhouse was created, which hoisted its flag for the first time in the autumn nine months later. This was the Globe, most famous of all the playhouses, and the birthplace of most of Shakespeare's greatest plays.

II. The "Globe"

We nowadays are so used to the methods of our modern stages, with their splendid effects of artificial scenery and lighting, prepared in secret and revealed as if by magic from behind curtains, that we find it hard to believe a play put on without these special things could be equally exciting. Yet when Shakespeare put on his own plays at the Globe, they were just as effective then under the open sky as they are today behind footlights; it is only that the effects he used were different. A favourite one, for example, which used to thrill Elizabethan audiences to the marrow, and which for obvious reasons we never use today, was the shooting off of cannon: remember that in *Henry V,* at the end of King Henry's famous rally before the walls of Harfleur, the stirring final cry of "God for Harry, England, and Saint George!" was the signal for a magnificent cannonade outside, and the actual smell of gunpowder would have hung in the air during all the rest of the battle. Then there is the familiar stage direction "Enter with drums and colours . . ." We may have the colours nowadays, but we get very little of the excitement the Elizabethans expected from their drums; neither for that matter do we have our trumpets blowing fanfares full on the stage as they did. Ours are smuggled away behind—"trumpets small within", as Shakespeare

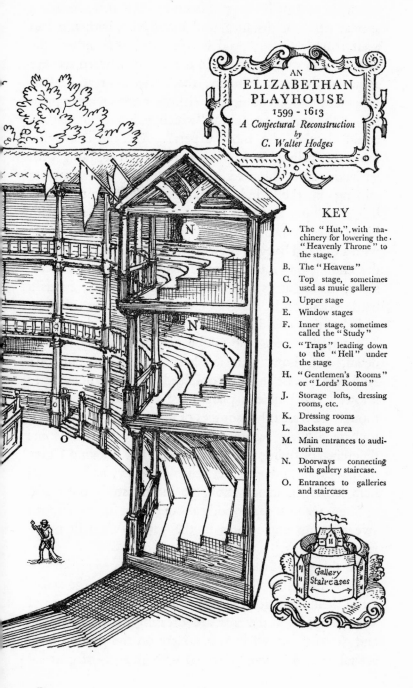

AN
ELIZABETHAN
PLAYHOUSE
1599 - 1613
A Conjectural Reconstruction
by
C. Walter Hodges

KEY

A. The "Hut," with machinery for lowering the "Heavenly Throne" to the stage.

B. The "Heavens"

C. Top stage, sometimes used as music gallery

D. Upper stage

E. Window stages

F. Inner stage, sometimes called the "Study"

G. "Traps" leading down to the "Hell" under the stage

H. "Gentlemen's Rooms" or "Lords' Rooms"

J. Storage lofts, dressing rooms, etc.

K. Dressing rooms

L. Backstage area

M. Main entrances to auditorium

N. Doorways connecting with gallery staircase.

O. Entrances to galleries and staircases

Gallery
Staircases

put it, in one of his stage directions; but that was for a special effect of distance, and usually his audience had their trumpets big. And besides this, although at the Globe there was not much in the way of painted scenery as we understand it today, there was a great deal of ornament and decoration. Visitors were much impressed by the wooden columns "which, painted like marble, could deceive the most expert". We must imagine the stage, painted as gay as a fair or a circus, hung with garlands and coloured tapestries and with banners stirring in the wind. Shakespeare's audience loved bright colours and rich dresses, spectacular scenes with kings on high thrones, devils springing out of trap-doors with a fizz and bang of fireworks, and gods and goddesses descending on clouds from Heaven: they loved processions, drums, flags and fighting, and when there was a battle going on in the Globe on Bankside, the trumpets and shouting could be heard right across the river.

What, then, was the Globe playhouse really like, in detail, and how were Shakespeare's plays put on? And here it must be sadly confessed that we do not exactly know. The builder's plans have all been lost, and although we have other sources of information upon which to base a fairly accurate reconstruction, there is some difference of opinion about details. The drawing I give on pages 48 and 49 is as reliable as any, and with its help let us, in imagination, go in and study the place.

There seems to be nobody about except for an old man sweeping up apple-cores in the yard. We will go in round the back.

All this part of the building behind the stage is known as the "tiring-house", that is, the place where the actors attire themselves for the play. It is a whole mixture of what in today's theatres are dressing-rooms, "wings" and green-room, all in one. Here on the ground level are tables and benches covered with all sorts of gear for the actors. Here too, is the prompter's place (they called him the "bookholder") with his copy of the play lying ready on a stool. The principal actors had their own parts, with the cues to be followed, written out on little narrow rolls of paper, easy to carry in the hand, and some of these we may see lying on the tables. There are also some false beards and wigs—a wig was called "a hair"—and some simple kinds of make-up: flour, to whiten the faces of villains, ghosts and corpses; ink, for putting on wrinkles with a quill pen; and perhaps some fine brick-dust for reddening cheeks—though another method was simply to slap them a bit before making an entrance. Burnt cork and charcoal were also used, for black faces and shadows. Blood—and there was a lot of this spilt about in Elizabethan plays—was real blood, got from the butcher's. So we may also see a basin or two of water and some pitchers, for cleaning up. There will of course be some looking-glasses, but not many and quite small, for they were expensive; and not very good, for they were difficult to make. But looking around, what a wonderful collection of dresses we find stored here in every corner! The Elizabethan stage was renowned for the splendour and extravagance of its attire. Here stuffed in baskets, there hanging along the wall, are the fantastic accoutrements of Roman and Turkish guise, pageant armour crested and painted, apparel for gods and goddesses, ghosts and devils, nymphs, heroes and fairies, a "cloak for to go invisible" and "a doublet of white satin laid thick with gold lace"— this last being but one of a multitude of rich courtly clothes which the players used to buy at second-hand from the wardrobes of noblemen and dandies, those "feathered estriches" who wore their fortunes on their backs. Besides all this, here, too, are stage "properties" of every imaginable kind. Thrones, tombs, caves, a "Hell Mouth", and "*Item,* 1 wooden canopy; old Mahomet's head.

Item, 1 lion skin; 1 bear's skin; and Phaeton's limbs and Phaeton's chariot; and Argus's head.

Item, Neptune's fork and garland.

Item, 1 crosier staff; Kent's wooden leg."

The above is quoted from a list of Henslowe's effects as given in his own diary; but it will do equally well for the property-room of the Globe. The list goes on and on, quoting at random a tree of golden apples, Mercury's wings, two coffins, a dragon, a "Cloth of the Sun and Moon" and many other things, including "a frame for the heading", which was a piece of trick machinery to give the illusion of someone being beheaded.

Much of this is stored in the space underneath the stage, where, bending our heads a little, we now make our way along. This, following the old custom of the medieval Mystery Plays, is known as the "Hell", and here are two trap-doors, through which ghosts and devils can be made to rise up on to the stage. We open one, knocking away the post that supports it from beneath, and climb through. The stage, where we now find ourselves, is large and high, and is surrounded by a railing. At the back leading into the tiring-house are two doors and, between them, a large recess which can be closed with a pair of curtains. This is in constant use during performances, for here are staged the occasional "set pieces" which require preparation while the play is going on out in front: the king's throne, or the table for a banquet, can be set here and "discovered" by the drawing aside of the curtains when ready. Above this recess we see a gallery, flanked by two openings called windows. This gallery is one of the most typical and useful features of the Elizabethan stage, and serves variously for an upper room as in the beginning of *The Taming of the Shrew,* or the poop of a ship or, most common of all, the battlements of a castle or town; and as for the windows, it is at one of these that Juliet appears while Romeo watches her from the "orchard" below. Now looking higher still, we see one other gallery. It is covered by a blue curtain patterned with stars to represent the sky, and it is usually supposed to be a part of "the Heavens", the name given to all the upper part of the stage, and particularly to the stage roof, the under side of which is richly decorated with paintings of the sun, moon and stars, and the signs of the Zodiac. Gods and goddesses are sometimes presented throned in glory in this high gallery: but today, when we climb up there by a ladder in the tiring-house, we find only some benches with sheets of music and instruments all ready, for the place is often used as a music gallery. Coming from here, unseen behind the starry curtain, the music can be made to have an effect of magic, of being in the air; for example, when, in *The Tempest,* Prospero magically summons his "heavenly music", it is from up here in the Heavens that it sounds.

There is one more ladder, leading to the highest part of all, the hut over the top of the stage. In here we find the winding gear which lets down the flying chariot in which the gods descend to earth. As has been said before this was a popular feature of many Elizabethan shows, but the descent had its mechanical difficulties: the machine creaked, and the noise had to be disguised by the "airy music", or better still by peals of thunder, most effectively produced by rolling cannon balls up and down on the wooden floor of the hut.

There is a door at the side of the hut, leading out to the little balcony from which they hoist the flag, and as we stand out here, looking over the thatched roof, we see to our surprise that an audience is assembling in the playhouse below. The players, we find, have suddenly returned, the musicians are tuning up their instruments, and one of them, trumpet in hand, is coming up here to blow the first sounding from our balcony. Let us go down quickly and find a good place to watch the play.

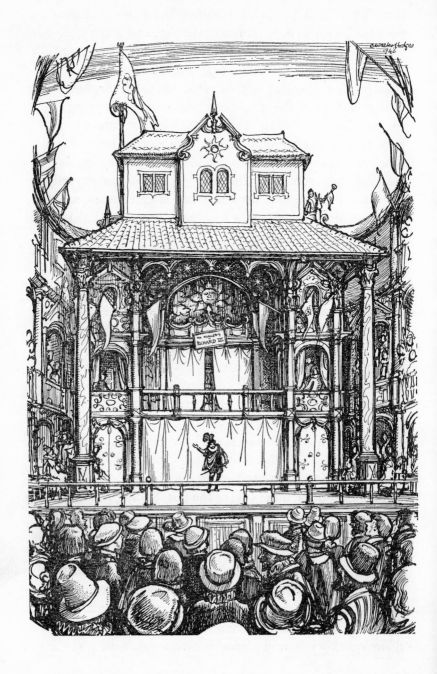

12. *A Performance of* Richard III

The play to be performed is Shakespeare's *Richard III,* in which Richard Burbage made such a great success when it was first performed eight years since. He is to appear again this afternoon in the title role, and, although it is an old play, big crowds have come to see him. The place is full everywhere, from the Lord's Rooms to the yard, and we were lucky to find a seat where our view of the back of the stage is not obscured by either of the two big pillars supporting the Heavens. Now, at the second sounding, a number of dandies come out from the tiring-house with stools in their hands, and seat themselves out of the way at the sides of the stage. It is rather a hot afternoon, and already it is getting a bit stuffy—even a bit smelly—in here: perhaps when the play starts . . . but there goes the third sounding, and there—enormous applause!—Burbage, as Richard of Gloucester, steps through the curtains on to the stage to begin the play.

On the following pages are sketches of some of the scenes from *Richard III* as they might have appeared that afternoon at the Globe.

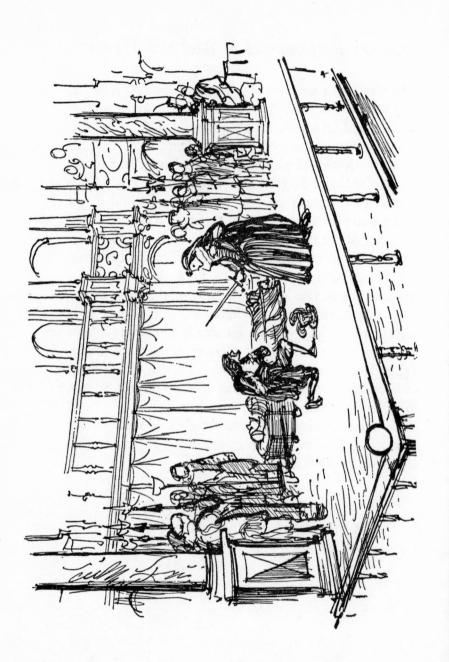

Richard III: Act I, Scene ii

*Enter the corpse of King Henry the Sixth, Gentlemen with halberds to
guard it; Lady Anne being the mourner.*

ANNE. *Set down, set down your honourable load—*
If honour may be shrouded in a hearse—
Whilst I awhile obsequiously lament
The untimely fall of virtuous Lancaster.
Poor key-cold figure of a holy king!
Pale ashes of the house of Lancaster! ...

Thus the scene is set, not with painted scenery, but
with the royal hearse, the halberds, the slow march, and
possibly also the slow beat of a drum and the tolling of a
bell. The Lady Anne (the part is, of course, played here
by a boy) is the widow of King Henry's son Edward,
murdered by the crookbacked Richard of Gloucester,
who soon enters the stage. The picture shows the
moment where he admits that he is the murderer of the
old King Henry also, and offers to let her kill him:

[*He lays his breast open: she offers at it with his sword.*

Nay, do not pause, for I did kill King Henry,
But 'twas thy beauty that provoked me
Nay, now dispatch; 'twas I that stabbed young Edward,
But 'twas thy heavenly face that set me on.

[*Here she lets fall the sword.*

Richard III: Act I, Scene iv

The stage now represents a place in the Tower of London, where the Duke of Clarence is a prisoner. While he sleeps, there enter the two murderers sent by his brother Richard.

SECOND MURDERER. *Come, shall we to this gear?*

FIRST MURDERER. *Take him over the costard with the hilts of thy sword, and then we will chop him in the malmsey-butt in the next room.*

SECOND MURDERER. *O excellent device! Make a sop of him!*

FIRST MURDERER. *Hark, he stirs: shall I strike?*

SECOND MURDERER. *No, first let's reason with him.*

(Fatal weakness for a professional murderer! The Duke reasons too well, and the Second Murderer's conscience begins to stir. In the end it is the First Murderer alone who takes the Duke over the costard.)

FIRST MURDERER. *Take that and that: if all this will not do, I'll drown you in the malmsey-butt within.*

[Exit, with the body.

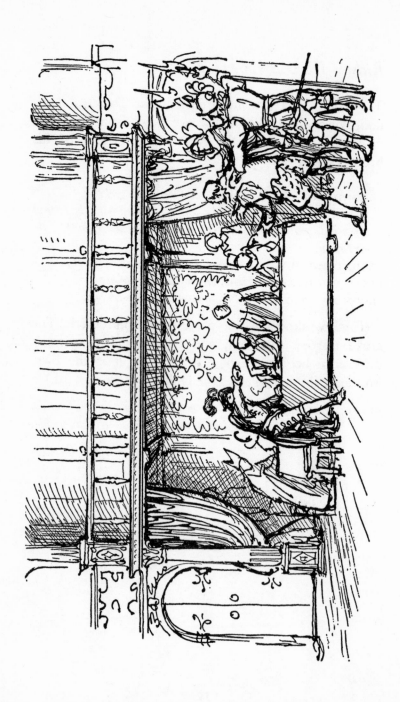

Richard III: Act III, Scene v

Enter BUCKINGHAM, DERBY, HASTINGS, THE BISHOP OF ELY, RATCLIFFE, LOVEL, *with others, and take their seats at a table.*

Lord Hastings, who has refused to take part in Richard's machinations to make himself king, is in the toils. Richard comes to the Council to denounce him on a trumped-up charge of witchcraft, and has him hustled off to immediate death:

> *Off with his head!   Now, by Saint Paul I swear*
> *I will not dine till I have seen the same.*

This picture shows one of the ways in which the curtained part at the back of the stage was used. The table, which has to be a long one to seat all these people, has been set ready on the inner stage during the preceding scene, and is now revealed by opening the curtains. It has also been carried forward a few paces (by two or three of the less important actors) so as to be better in view of all parts of the auditorium. When the scene is over, the table will be quickly withdrawn and the curtains closed again.

C. WALTER HODGES

Richard III: Act III, Scene vii

Richard's plot is on the point of success, and he is now ready to make himself king; but it is none the less necessary for him to seem unwilling to take the throne except at the earnest entreaty of the common people. The Duke of Buckingham, having contrived to work some of the common people into the right frame of mind, brings them with the Lord Mayor to Baynard's Castle, where Richard is waiting. Then:

> *Enter* RICHARD *aloft, between two Bishops.*
>
> MAYOR. *See where he stands between two clergymen!*
> BUCKINGHAM. *Two props of virtue for a Christian prince* . . .

"Alas," protests Richard, when the crown is offered:

> *Why would you heap these cares on me?*
> *I am unfit for State and majesty.*

In the foreground Catesby, Richard's follower, smiles behind his hand.

The sketch shows a common use of the upper stage, which here represents the walls of Baynard's Castle. It is quite likely, although I have not shown it, that some form of painted scenery representing battlements may sometimes have been used on these occasions, instead of the railing.

The figures which can be seen at the windows at either side of the upper stage are part of the audience. There is a big crowd and all the auditorium is full, so the stage windows have been let out as additional "boxes".

Richard III: Act IV, Scene ii

The costumes being worn in this play are more or less those of Shakespeare's own time. This may make it difficult in the sketch opposite to sort out the players from the audience. Those standing in the background are players, members of Richard's court who have withdrawn to allow him to talk privately with Buckingham. Those seated are audience.

So Richard has become king, though he still does not feel secure enough on his ill-gotten throne:

Ha! am I King? 'tis so: but Edward lives.

He means to take the life of the young prince Edward and his brother, and intends that Buckingham shall help him. But Buckingham recoils from such a crime—and later pays with his own head for his scruples.

Notice the throne. This, sometimes called a "State", is a very hard-worked piece of Elizabethan stage furniture. Richard's throne today will be used by Tamburlaine or Julius Cæsar tomorrow. Perhaps a playhouse would possess two or three different thrones, but regular patrons would soon know all the customary stage properties by heart, and would be sure to notice whenever a new piece was added or an old one came out in a new coat of paint and freshly gilded, for some special play.

Richard III: Act V, Scene ii

Enter RICHMOND, OXFORD, BLUNT, HERBERT *and others, with drum and colours.*

There is in another of Shakespeare's plays a stage direction which reads: "Drum and colours: Enter . . . the whole army." Perhaps the stage army which mustered more than some nine or ten souls, except on very special occasions, would have been lucky. In *Henry V* Shakespeare begs pardon of the audience for the small forces he is about to deploy on so splendid and legendary a battle as Agincourt:

> *And so our scene must to the battle fly*
> *Where—O for pity;—we shall much disgrace*
> *With four or five most vile and ragged foils*
> *Right ill-disposed in brawl ridiculous*
> *The name of Agincourt.*

But surely this was an apology in form only. The entry of the stage army, with its drum and colours and flourish of trumpets, must have been as much looked forward to on an Elizabethan stage as is Cinderella's coach in a Christmas pantomime today, and as much applauded when at last it came marching on.

In this play the sound of Richmond's drum is the sound of retribution overtaking King Richard in the end, marching to Bosworth Field.

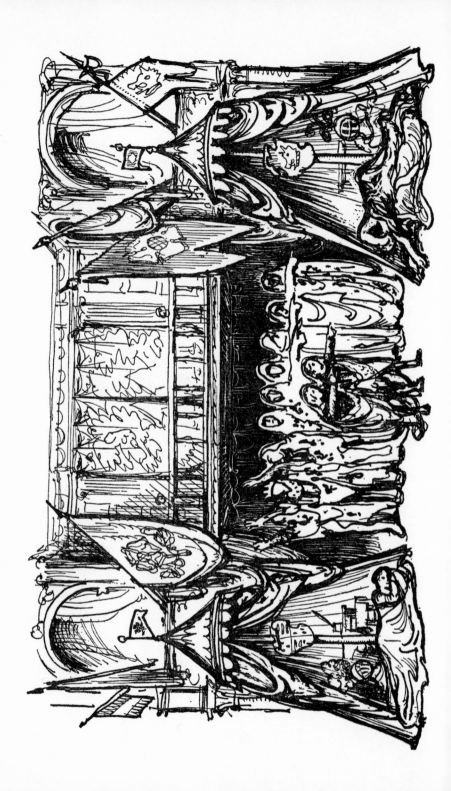

Richard III: Act V, Scene ii

Enter KING RICHARD *in arms, with* NORFOLK, THE EARL OF
SURREY, *and others.*

RICHARD. *Here pitch our tents, even here in Bosworth Field* . . .

So Richard's tent is put up on one side of the stage, and
a little while later:

Enter, on the other side of the field, RICHMOND, SIR WILLIAM
BRANDON, OXFORD, *and others. Some of the soldiers pitch
Richmond's tent.*

The two tents, one on each side, with their flags
disposed about them, represent the opposing armies. The
stage between is Bosworth Field. Each in his own tent,
the two leaders make their plans for the morrow and then
lie down to rest.

The ghosts of Richard's eleven victims now come forth
to haunt him in his sleep. "Despair and die!" they cry
to him, while to Richmond they promise quiet sleep and
happy victory.

> *God and good angels fight on Richmond's side;*
> *And Richard falls in height of all his pride.*
> [*The ghosts vanish.* RICHARD *starts out of his dream.*

How this was actually done we can only guess. In the
picture the ghosts are shown draped in their blood-
stained shrouds. Each, after he has spoken, steps back
a few paces into the inner stage, which stands open
all hung around with black. Then, as Richard starts up
awake, the curtains are quickly closed over the inner
stage, and the ghosts are no more seen.

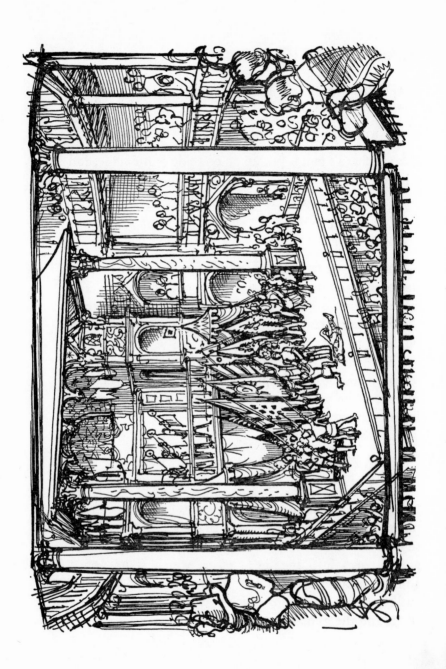

Richard III: *Act V, Scene v*

Alarum. Enter RICHARD *and* RICHMOND; *they fight.* RICHARD
is slain. Retreat and flourish. Re-enter RICHMOND, DERBY
bearing the crown, with divers other Lords.

RICHMOND. *God and your arms be praised, victorious friends!*
          The day is ours; the bloody dog is dead.

DERBY.   *Courageous Richmond, well hast thou acquit thee.*
          Lo, here, this long usurped royalty
          From the dead temples of this bloody wretch
          Have I pluck'd off, to grace thy brows withal:
          Wear it, enjoy it, and make much of it!

RICHMOND. *Great God of heaven, say amen to all!*

13. Stage Music

It was said on an earlier page that an Elizabethan play-goer would speak of going to the theatre to *hear* a play, not, as we do, to *see* one. "I will hear that play," says Duke Theseus in *A Midsummer Night's Dream,* when he is told about the clowns' "tedious brief scene" of Pyramus and Thisbe; and he insists again: "We will hear it." The very word "audience" means a group of hearers. We should remember, too, that since Elizabethan plays were written in verse, and were therefore obviously not intended to be realistic representations of everyday life and speech, they could be said to be a sort of music-drama or opera—that is, if you will agree that verse itself is a sort of music in words. And so, as if to continue this idea, music itself was brought into the drama in its own right, with ever-increasing elegance and effect, to support the action on the stage.

The musical instruments of that time, as of our own, were divided into their two main families, of stringed instruments and wind instruments. Unlike the practice of our own time, however, it was not usual to combine these two families in one orchestra. Because the character of stringed and wind instruments was so dissimilar it was thought best to combine each kind only into bands or "consorts" on their own. This was sensible also because their respective strength of sound was very unequal; the strings of those days had only a gentle sound, and were no match for the wind. (However, there were odd occasions when strings and wind *were* combined, and a band of this sort was known as a "broken consort".)

Their wind instruments were trumpets and cornets, sackbuts (which were an early form of trombone),

Lute

Shawms & Hautboys

Cittern

Sackbut

Viols

Viol-de-Gamba

Recorders

and hunting horns. All these were loud and flaring instruments of a military character. Their wood-winds were hautboys and shawms (both ancestors of the modern oboe), which gave out a rather gay, brilliant note; and the whole family of recorders, the same as they are today. Trumpets and hautboys, which had powerful voices and could be played while standing or marching, were very suitable for music out of doors, and so they were naturally the instruments most used in the open-air public theatres.

The stringed instruments were: viols, which were early forms of the violin (the word "fiddles" was already in use for them, as also was a strange now unfamiliar word, "crowds"); the viol-da-gamba, an early form of the cello; and several kinds of guitar-like instruments, of which the most common were the cittern and the lute. The lute was the most beautiful, versatile and expressive instrument of the age. To play it well with all its sixteen strings required a skilled lutanist; but it was a skill practised by many people, especially among the actors.

The stringed instruments with their gentler voices were best suited to the small indoor theatres, which were patronised by the more educated and fashionable audiences. So it was in these "private" playhouses that the art of dramatic music now began to be developed. It was here that the gallery at the back over the stage first began to be known as "the music room", since here the musicians had a more or less permanent place. Here, too, there began the custom of having musical interludes between the acts of a play, which was never done in the great open-air theatres on Bankside.

A band of wind musicians was known as "the waits", an old word derived from the waiting sentinel of the watch in ancient times, who was recognised by the blowing of his horn. A consort of strings was called, rather oddly, a "noise". One of these, called "Sneak's noise" (being led by a man named Sneak), was well known in Shakespeare's London, and is mentioned in his play of *Henry IV*, where the servants at the Boar's Head Tavern are sent out to fetch it, to make a merry evening for Falstaff's friends. Well-known waits and noises could be hired for weddings, and supper parties and other such occasions, and doubtless they sometimes helped out at the theatres as well. Most of the players' companies, however, had their own musicians. They had to be able to play some quite complicated trumpet calls, if nothing else. There were "tuckets" and "flourishes" and "alarums", all of which were different, and there was a "sennet", which appears to have been a long ceremonial trumpet-piece, perhaps specially composed, to accompany a solemn procession.

Some of the actors were especially well known for their singing and lute-playing. Boy players in particular were recruited for their musical abilities. In *Much Ado About Nothing* there is a boy called (in the play) Balthasar, who has to sing the song "Sigh no more, Ladies". But it seems that the first copy of the play sent to the printer had some special back-stage notes written in it, and these were printed into the edition by mistake: so in one place "Balthasar" is suddenly called "Jack Wilson", who as we happen to know, was a boy of fourteen, apprenticed to the Company. Jack Wilson was probably the same young actor who took the part of the boy Lucius in the first production of *Julius Cæsar*. If so it was he who played the lute and sang to Brutus in his tent on the night before the battle of Philippi. His was the sad music that crept round the hushed galleries of the Globe, bringing in a still and solemn mood, till Lucius falls asleep over his lute, and the ghost of Cæsar appears upon the stage: "Ha! Who comes here?" demands Brutus, and the ghost replies: "Thy evil spirit, Brutus."

So a mood and a scene were created by music. Again

and again throughout Shakespeare's plays one finds music used as a background for this purpose: at the beginning of *Twelfth Night*, to set the scene for the lovesick Count; or to make a sad quiet wakening for mad old King Lear when he is found by his only loving daughter at last; or for a magical singing in the air when Ferdinand and Miranda meet and fall in love, in *The Tempest*.

The English in those days were famous for their music. Their composers were the best in Europe, and their published songs were bought by ordinary families who, so we are told, used to bring out their part-books after supper and sit round the table singing together. Even in the barbers' shops a cittern was provided for customers to play, while waiting to be shaved. And now ordinary citizens of Elizabethan London, eager for music, could hear it played by professional players and singers in their famous playhouses, most days of the week. It was an opportunity they did not let slip.

14. *Essex's Rebellion*

The Globe first opened its doors in the autumn of 1599, and one of the new plays presented there that season was Shakespeare's *Julius Cæsar*. Earlier that summer, at the Curtain, next door to the now vacant site of the old Theatre, there had been a first performance of his *Henry V,* and in the course of that play he had introduced a compliment to the great Earl of Essex who was then in Ireland waging (as Shakespeare did not know) a most feeble and unsuccessful war. Shakespeare looked forward to the Earl's victorious return, "bringing rebellion broached on his sword", and ventured to compare it with Henry V's triumphant return after Agincourt.

Alas, it came out very differently. There was more applause for the opening of the new playhouse that September than for the homecoming of the Earl. He brought nothing with him but an almost treacherous peace, and a following of adventurers and malcontents whose ambitions he had encouraged as a support for other, more overweening, ambitions of his own. During all the following year, perceiving that he could never again become, as once he had been, the favourite of the old Queen, he found himself sinking deeper and deeper into the mire of a conspiracy, his own, to overthrow her. By the beginning of 1601 the situation in London was critical. The Earl, in his palace by the river, was hesitating on the brink of open rebellion. The Queen, knowing that he was as rash as he was popular, cautiously bided her time and waited for him to make a false step.

On the 6th of February, 1601, a Friday, there came into the tiring-house of the Globe a certain Sir Gilly Meyricke, with some of his friends, all ardent supporters of the Earl of Essex. They wanted to persuade the players to change whatever plans they had for the following afternoon, and put on a performance of Shakespeare's *Richard II* instead. The players were unwilling. They explained that, with all the uneasiness of the time, they were having a bad season, that *Richard II* was an old play which was out of fashion and would not draw, and they could not risk losing money by playing it to an empty house. But Sir Gilly and his friends were very pressing. They declared they would pay in advance enough money to cover the day's takings, in addition to whatever else the players could take at the door in the ordinary way. This was a good offer, and with a little more persuasion the players accepted it. Perhaps the knight and his party stayed a little longer to explain how they wanted some certain details of the play to be brought out. Did the players suspect what was behind it all?

The point was that the story of Richard II, represented as an unworthy English sovereign turned off the throne by a popular hero, had become peculiarly linked up in people's minds with the fortunes of Essex, and in the brewing crisis Sir Gilly Meyricke's act was generally understood as an act of encouragement to the Earl's supporters and of barely concealed defiance to the Queen. Did the players understand this when they took the bribe —for that, in effect, was what it was? At least they must have had their qualms that Saturday during the performance, with Sir Gilly and all his host of friends so eagerly acclaiming every line that pointed to the deserved overthrow of a king. How relieved they must have been when the anxious afternoon passed off without incident, and their dangerous patrons had returned again over the river to the bustle of excited expectation that hung about the courtyard of Essex House.

The next morning the storm burst. The Earl marched into the City at the head of his cheering supporters to raise the citizens against the Queen. The citizens shut their doors. Soon the cheering grew less loud and the Earl's supporters remarkably less numerous. By late afternoon the citizens came out of doors again to gossip about the great fiasco; and on Bankside that evening, from the roof of the Globe, the players might have seen a little boat going up river, taking the Earl ignominiously home to Essex House. Or, next day, they might have seen the barge pass by that took him back again down river to the Tower.

The players were questioned about that suspicious Saturday performance, but nothing was held against them. They could not be blamed because a patron had paid them to act a well-known play. Evil was in the eye of the beholder.

Just a fortnight later, on the evening of the 24th of February, they were summoned to act at Court. Perhaps the Master of the Revels had been advised to provide some distraction for the Queen, to keep her from thinking too much about the days, not very long past, when Essex had been her devoted favourite and the hero of her Court. We do not know what performance the players gave that night, and we may well wonder how much of it the aged Queen listened to as she sat there with the candle-light twinkling on her rich clothes.

Essex was beheaded next morning.

15. *Ben Jonson and Others*

In 1603 King James I came to the throne. Shakespeare by this time was a well-to-do man, owner of a large house in his home town in Warwickshire, and entitled to his own coat of arms. He was William Shakespeare, gentleman, of Stratford-upon-Avon; poet, playwright, player, and "Master-Sharer" of the Globe; and his company was now honoured by the new King with the title of "The King's Men". King James proved to be an enthusiastic patron of all forms of theatrical entertainment, and the players now flourished more than ever before. This was the period when Shakespeare wrote his four great tragedies, *Hamlet, Othello, King Lear* and *Macbeth*—a play with a Scottish setting, in compliment to the nationality of the new King.

But Shakespeare was now no longer without his rivals. Greatest of these was (and still is) Benjamin Jonson. He was a big, brilliant, quarrelsome man. As a youth he had been a soldier, fighting against the Spaniards in the Netherlands. In later life he escaped

hanging only by a hair-breadth, after he had killed a bully in a duel; he got away with the punishment of being branded on his left thumb with the letter T—for Tyburn, the place of common execution. It was said that Shakespeare was the first to recognise his genius as a playwright. Jonson had shown his play *Every Man in his Humour* to Burbage, who had refused it; but Shakespeare, having called Jonson back, read the play himself, and persuaded Burbage to change his mind. Shakespeare himself took a part in it when it was performed. It proved to be one of the greatest of English comedies. Others that Jonson wrote are *The Alchemist* and *The Silent Woman*.

Besides Ben Jonson there were now so many well-

known playwrights that there is no room here to mention
more than a few by name. But let us, for a moment,
join a group of them at supper at the Mermaid Tavern
in Cheapside in, say, the year 1604. It is April the 23rd,
Shakespeare's fortieth birthday, and his friends have
invited him to a celebration. Shakespeare is at the head
of the table; on his right, Richard Burbage has risen to
propose his health; on his left sits Ben Jonson; next to
Jonson is Thomas Dekker, who wrote the play *The
Shoemaker's Holiday*. (He also wrote an interesting book
about the life and tricks of thieves and beggars in London,
from which I quoted a little earlier on.) Opposite
him sits Thomas Heywood, who claimed to have had a

hand in the writing of more than two hundred plays. Next is John Webster, author of the *Duchess of Malfi*; next again, John Marston (who might not have come here to supper had he known Ben Jonson was here, for the two had been publicly quarrelling for years about each other's plays); and at the end of the table Francis Beaumont and John Fletcher, the famous partnership of friends who lived and worked together and were joint authors, among much else, of *The Knight of the Burning Pestle*.

In the background is Master Sneak of "Sneak's Noise", playing the lute in a "broken consort".

16. *The Court Masques*

It was Ben Jonson who was chiefly responsible for the return to fashion of the Court Masque. This was rather like a stately pantomime or charade, arranged with poetry, dancing, music, and elaborate scenery and dresses, for the private pleasure of the King and his Court. The principal parts were often taken by members of the royal family, or by courtiers, though sometimes professional players were employed as well. It was not a new form of entertainment, but under the patronage of King James it now took on a new and splendid lease of life. Many thousands of pounds would be spent for a masque for one night.

Ben Jonson proved to have a special talent for devising this kind of show, and he was fortunate in having to work with a partner as brilliant as himself. This was Inigo Jones, who was not only a great architect, but had also, while travelling in Italy, copied the new types of theatrical scenery and effects which were being developed there. Many of his designs for these Court Masques

have been preserved, and the scenery shown in the picture on page 83 is based upon some of them.

It shows the masque of *Oberon, the Faery Prince*, which was produced by Jonson and Inigo Jones on New Year's Day, 1611. It was given in The Banqueting Hall at Westminster, in honour of Henry, Prince of Wales, who probably himself took the part of Oberon. This show opened in front of a "cliff", before which some "Sylvans and Satyrs" appeared. After the action had gone a little way the "cliff" parted in the middle and drew back, revealing the outside of a fairy castle. There followed an "antick dance", which ended suddenly with the crowing of a cock; and upon this the castle itself opened, showing inside a scene in fairyland, with Oberon the Faery Prince mounted in a chariot drawn by two white bears, and attended by all his Court.

From now on for nearly forty years, that is until the outbreak of the Civil War, not a winter passed at White-hall palace without one or more of these gorgeous entertainments taking place. However, it is possible to suppose that not everything, not even at the King's Court, always went off without a hitch. On page 100 you will find an account, written at the time, of one masque that suddenly took a wrong turning.

The growing fashion for masques can be seen reflected in most of Shakespeare's later plays. They are plays of fantasy and romance, and were staged with more elaborate dresses and effects than Shakespeare had been accustomed to use in earlier days. In *Cymbeline* there is a scene where Jupiter descends from the Heavens on an eagle; in *Pericles* there is a pageant boat on wheels which is "sailed" in through the yard and moored alongside the stage; and in *The Tempest*, his last play, there is included a masque in which nymphs and shepherds and goddesses come forth to celebrate the betrothal of Ferdinand and Miranda.

17. *Shakespeare goes Home*

On the 29th of June, 1613, there was presented at the
Globe a new play about Henry VIII. It may have been
Shakespeare's own play; but whether this was so or not,
the performance that day was never finished. What
happened is told in a letter written by a certain Sir
Henry Wotton to his nephew, a few days later:

"Now, to let matters of state sleep, I will entertain you
at the present with what has happened this week at the
Bank's side. The King's Players had a new play called
All is True, representing some principal pieces of the
reign of Henry VIII, which was set forth with many
extraordinary circumstances of pomp and majesty.
. . . Now, King Henry making a masque at the Cardinal
Wolsey's house, and certain chambers[1] being shot off at
his entry, some of the paper, or other stuff, wherewith one
of them was stopped, did light on the thatch, where being
thought at first but an idle smoke, and their eyes more
attentive to the show, it kindled inwardly and ran round
like a train, consuming within less than an hour the
whole house to the very grounds. . . . Yet nothing did
perish but wood and straw, and a few forsaken cloaks;
only one man had his breeches set on fire, that would
perhaps have broiled him, if he had not by the benefit of a
provident wit put it out with bottle ale."

So ended the Globe.   Or, rather, so ended the timbers
of the old Theatre: for the Globe was rebuilt and open
again by the following summer, by all accounts more
splendid than before.

And with the burning of the first Globe we may end
our short account of Shakespeare and his theatre.   For

[1] *i.e.* cannons.

85

some years he had been spending more and more of his time at his home in Stratford, quietly assuming the dignities of a well-to-do citizen. By the time the Globe was burned he was not often seen in London. Quite suddenly, three years later, on his fifty-second birthday, he died. He was buried at Stratford.

But for our last picture of him let us see him at home in his garden on a summer's evening a few years before. With him are his daughter Susanna, her husband and their little girl; and his younger daughter Judith.

He has been writing, and now it is supper-time; they have come to help him to carry in his things.

The Players: An Anthology

1. What learn You by That?

An extract from the pamphlet Plays Confuted In Five Actions *written in 1582 by the puritan Stephen Gosson to demonstrate that play-acting was a vain, silly and immoral occupation.*

Sometime you shall see nothing at a play but the adventures of an amourous knight, passing from country to country for the love of his lady, encountering many a terrible monster made of brown paper, and at his return is so wonderfully changed, that he cannot be known but by a broken ring, or a handkercher, or a piece of a cockle shell. *What learn you by that?* . . . If any goodness were to be learned at plays it is likely that the players themselves, which commit every syllable to memory, should profit most. But the daily experience of their behaviour showeth that they reap no profit by the discipline themselves.

2. Troubles at the "Theatre"

An extract from a report upon brawls and disturbances at the Theatre, sent to Lord Burghley by the Recorder of the City of London in June 1584. The "stubborn Fellow" in the last paragraph, who refused to answer his summons, was James Burbage.

Upon Monday night I returned to London and found all the wards of the City full of watchers. The cause thereof was for that very near the Theatre or Curtain, at the time of the plays, there lay a prentice sleeping upon the grass,

Trouble was not uncommon at the playhouses. Shown here is a riot which took place in 1602 when a dishonest manager ran off with the gate-money, without providing a play. He was caught in the end; but meanwhile the angry audience had "made great spoil" of the theatre.

and one Challes, alias Grostock, did turn upon the toe upon the belly of the same prentice, whereupon the apprentice started up, and after words they fell to plain blows. The company increased of both sides to the number of five hundred at the least. This Challes exclaimed and said that he was a gentleman and that the apprentice was but a rascal; and he said the prentices were but the scum of the world. Upon these troubles the prentices began the next day, being Tuesday, to make mutinies and assemblies, and did conspire to have broken the prisons and to have taken forth the prentices that were imprisoned; but my Lord and I, having intelligence thereof, apprehended four or five of the chief conspirators, who are in Newgate and stand indicted.

Upon Wednesday one Browne, a serving man in a blue coat, a shifting fellow having a perilous wit of his own, intending a robbery if he could have brought it to pass, did at Theatre door quarrel with certain poor boys, handicraft prentices, and struck some of them, and lastly he with his sword wounded and maimed one of the boys upon the left hand; whereupon there assembled near a thousand people. This Browne did very cunningly convey himself away, but by chance he was caught later, and brought to Mr. Humphrey Smith; but because no man was able to charge him he dismissed him. And after this Browne was brought before Mr. Yonge, where he defended himself so cunningly and subtly, no man being there to charge him, that there also he was dismissed. After this I sent a warrant for him, and the constables with the deputy found him at the Bell in Holborn, in a parlour fast locked in; and he would not obey the warrant, but with the help of the innkeeper he was conveyed away. Then I sent for the innkeeper and caused him to appear at Newgate, at the Sessions, where he was committed until he brought forth his guest. The next day he brought him forth, and so we indicted him for his misdemeanour. This Browne is a common cozener, a thief and a horse stealer. He resteth now in Newgate.

Upon Wednesday, Thursday, Friday and Saturday we did nothing else but sit in commission and examine these misdemeanours. Upon Sunday my Lord sent two Aldermen to the Court for the suppressing and pulling down of the Theatre and Curtain. All the lords agreed thereunto, saving my Lord Chamberlain and Mr. Vice-Chamberlain, but we obtained a letter to suppress them all. Upon the same night I sent for the Queen's players and my Lord of Arundel his players, and they all willingly obeyed the Lord's letters. The chiefest of her Highness' players advised me to send for the owner of the Theatre who is a stubborn fellow, and to bind him on oath to obey. I did so; but he sent me word that he was my Lord of Hunsdon's man, and that he would not come to me, but he would in the morning ride to Lord Hunsdon. Then I sent the undersheriff for him, and he brought him to me; and at his coming he shouted me out very hasty; and in the end I shewed him his master, Lord Hunsdon's, letter and signature and then he was more quiet; but to die for it he would not be bound. And then I being of a mind to send him to prison, he made suit that he might be bound to appear at the Court of Oier and Determiner, which is tomorrow; where he said that he was sure the Court would not bind him, being a Counsellers' man. And so I have granted his request, where he shall be sure to be bound, or else is like to do worse.

3. The Players a Public Nuisance

The Lord Mayor of London writes to the Archbishop of Canterbury, seeking his help to diminish the protection which the Queen and her Court give to the players, so that they can be prevented from playing in the City.

Whereas by the daily and disorderly exercise of a number of players and playing houses erected within this city, the youth thereof is greatly corrupted and their manners infected with many evil and ungodly qualities, by reason of the wanton and profane devices represented on the stages by the said players, the prentices and servants withdrawn from their works, and all sorts in general from the daily resort unto sermons and other Christian exercises, we most humbly beseech your Grace to vouchsafe us your good favour and help for the reforming and banishing of so great evil out of this city, which ourselves of long time (though to small purpose) have so earnestly desired and endeavoured by all means that possibly we could. And because we understand that the Queen's Majesty must be served at certain times by this sort of people, we are most humbly and earnestly to beseech your Grace to call unto you the Master of Her Majesty's Revels, and to treat with him, if by any means it may be devised that Her Majesty may be served with these recreations as hath been accustomed (which in our opinions may easily be done) by the private exercise of Her Majesty's own players in convenient place, and the city freed from these continual disorders.

4. The Players as Gentle as Lambs

In 1594 the player company managed by Burbage, Shake-
speare and others came under the special protection of the
Queen's Chamberlain, Lord Henry Hunsdon. Here he
writes to the Lord Mayor making a polite but firm request
for the players to be allowed to play at one of the great inns
within the City of London. There had been a bad plague
epidemic for the two previous years, but this had now passed
over.

Whereas my now company of Players have been accustomed for the better exercise of their quality, and for the service of her Majesty if need so require, to play this winter time within the City at the Cross Keys in Gracious Street, this is to require and pray your Lordship (the time being such as, thanks be to God, there is now no danger of the sickness) to permit and suffer them so to do; which I pray you the rather to do since they have undertaken to me that, where formerly they began not their plays till towards four o'clock, they will now being at two, and will have done between four and five, and will not use any drums or trumpets at all for the calling of people together, and shall be contributories to the poor of the parish where they play, according to their abilities. And so not doubting of your willingness to yield hereunto, upon these reasonable conditions, I commit you to the Almighty. At Nonesuch Palace, this 8th of October 1594.

Your lord's loving friend,

H. Hunsdon.

To my honorable good friend Sir Richard Martin, knight, Lord Mayor of the City of London.

5. To play in Plague-time . . .

The following is part of a letter from the City Council of London to the Queen's Privy Council at Westminster, written in 1584, pointing out the dangers of allowing crowds of people to gather at playhouses, even when infection of the plague was believed to be decreasing.

To play in plague-time is to increase the plague by infection: to play out of plague-time is to draw the plague by offendings of God upon occasion of such plays.

But touching the permission of plays upon the fewness of those that die in any week, it may please you to remember one special thing. In the report of the plague we report only those that die, and we make no report of those that recover and carry infection about them either in their sores running, or in their garments, which sort are the most dangerous. Now, my Lord, when the number of those that die grow fewest, the number of those that go abroad with sores is greatest, the violence of the disease to kill being abated. And therefore while any plague is to be found, though the number reported of them that die be small, the number infectious is so great that plays are not to be permitted.

6. Rogues and Vagabonds

From The Description of England, *by William Harrison, published in 1587.*

It is not yet full threescore years since this trade of rogues and vagabonds began, but how it hath prospered since that time it is easy to judge, for they are now supposed, of one sex and another, to amount unto above 10,000 persons, as I have heard reported.   Moreover, in counterfeiting the Egyptian rogues, they have devised a language among themselves, which they name "canting", or sometimes "pedlar's French", a speech composed thirty years since of English and a great number of odd words of their own devising, without order or reason, and yet such as none but themselves are able to understand.   The first deviser thereof was hanged by the neck—a just reward, no doubt, for his deserts, and a common end to all of that profession.

A gentleman, Thomas Harman, also of late hath taken great pains to search out the secret practices of this ungracious rabble.   And among other things he setteth down and describeth three and twenty sorts of them whose names it shall not be amiss to remember whereby each one may take occasion to read and know what wicked people they are, and what villainy remaineth in them.

The several disorders and degrees amongst our idle vagabonds.

1. Rufflers.	2. Uprightmen.
3. Hookers or anglers.	4. Rogues.
5. Wild rogues.	6. Priggers of prancers.
7. Palliards.	8. Fraters.
9. Abrams.	10. Freshwater mariners or whipjacks.
11. Dummerers.	12. Drunken tinkers.
13. Swadders or pedlars.	14. Jarkmen or patricoes.

Of the women kind.

1. Demanders for glimmer or fire.
2. Bawdy-baskets.
3. Morts.
4. Autem morts.
5. Walking morts.
6. Doxies.
7. Dells.
8. Kinching morts.
9. Kinching coes.

The punishment that is ordained for this kind of people is very sharp, and yet it cannot restrain them from their gadding: wherefore the end must needs be martial law, to be exercised upon them, as upon thieves, robbers, despisers of all laws, and enemies to the commonwealth and welfare of the land.

7. Bethsabe's Song *by George Peele*

At the opening of Peele's play David and Bethsabe, *the stage-direction is that "the Prologue-speaker, before going out, draws a curtain and discloses Bethsabe with her maid, bathing over a spring". She is supposed to be in a green leafy arbour, shaded from the sun. King David is seated at an upper window, secretly watching her. Bethsabe sings:*

Hot sun, cool fire, temper'd with sweet air,
Black shade, fair nurse, shadow my white hair:
Shine, sun; burn, fire; breathe, air, and ease me;
Black shade, fair nurse, shroud me, and please me:
Shadow, my sweet nurse, keep me from burning,
Make not my glad cause cause of my mourning.
　　　　Let not my beauty's fire
　　　　Inflame unstaid desire,
　　　　Nor pierce any bright eye
　　　　That wandereth lightly.

8. The Mermaid Tavern

From "Mr. Francis Beaumont's Letter to Ben Jonson".

... What things have we seen
Done at the Mermaid! heard words that have been
So nimble, and so full of subtile flame,
As if that everyone from whence they came
Had meant to put his whole wit in a jest,
And had resolved to live a fool the rest
Of his dull life; then when there hath been thrown
Wit able enough to justify the town
For three days past; wit that might warrant be
For the whole city to talk foolishly
Till that were cancell'd; and when that was gone,
We left an air behind us, which alone
Was able to make the two next companies
Right witty; though but downright fools, mere wise!

9. A Masque that went Wrong

This hilarious account of a feast given by King James I to celebrate a state visit by his brother-in-law the King of Denmark in July 1606, was written by Sir John Harington, who was tutor to the Prince of Wales. Harington had been a courtier noted for his wit in Queen Elizabeth's time, but he did not like the more dissolute ways of the court of King James. His chief fame today is that he was the inventor of the modern lavatory water-closet.

One day, a great feast was held, and, after dinner, the representation of Solomon his Temple and the coming of the Queen of Sheba was made, or (as I may better say) was meant to have been made, before their Majesties! by device of the Earl of Salisbury and others. But alas, As all earthly things do fail to poor mortals in enjoyment, so did prove our presentment hereof. The Lady who did play the Queen's part, did carry most precious gifts to both their Majesties; but forgetting the steps arising to the canopy, overset her caskets into his Danish Majesty's lap, and fell at his feet, though I rather think it was in his face. Much was the hurry and confusion; cloths and napkins were at hand, to make all clean. His Majesty then got up and would dance with the Queen of Sheba; but he fell down and humbled himself before her, and was carried to an inner chamber, and laid on a bed of state; which was not a little defiled with the presents of the Queen which had been bestowed on his garments; such as wine, cream, jelly, beverage, cakes, spices, and other good matters. The entertainment and show went forward, and most of the presenters went backward, or fell down; wine did so occupy their upper chambers. Now did appear, in rich dress, Hope, Faith, and Charity: Hope did essay to speak, but wine rendered her endeavours so feeble that she withdrew, and hoped the King would excuse her brevity; Faith was then all alone, for I am certain she was not joined with good works, and left the court in a staggering condition: Charity came to the King's feet, and seemed to cover the multitude of sins her sisters had committed; in some sort she made obeisance and brought gifts, but said she would return home again, as there was no gift which heaven had not already given his Majesty. She then returned to Hope and Faith, who were both sick and spewing in the lower hall. Next came Victory, in bright armour, and presented a rich sword to the King, who did not accept it, but put it by with his hand; and, by a strange medley of versification, did endeavour to make suit to the King. But Victory did not triumph long, for, after much lamentable utterance, she was led away like a silly captive, and laid to sleep in the outer steps of the ante-chamber. Now did Peace make entry, and strive to get foremost to the King; but I grieve to tell how great wrath she did discover unto those of her attendants; and, much contrary to her semblance, most rudely made war with her olive branch, and laid on the pates of those who did oppose her coming.

10. The Burning of the "Globe"

This popular ballad, called "A Sonnet upon the pitiful burning of the Globe playhouse in London", was printed and sold in the streets of London on the very next day after the fire. These notes about it may be of use: (i) Melpomene was the classical Muse of Tragedy hence her black (sea-coal) robe. (ii) "...and yet all this is true." All is True was given at the time as the title of the play about Henry the Eighth which caused the fire. (iii and iv) Henry Condye, or Condell, and "old stuttering Hemmings" were two of Shakespeare's closest actor friends, and a few years later became the editors of the famous "First Folio" of his collected Works. (v) The ale-house stood next door close to the Globe, and was burned with it. (vi) "...Expense for tiles." The players heeded this advice. When they rebuilt the Globe it was roofed with tiles, not thatch.

Now sit thee down, Melpomene,
   Wrapt in a sea-coal robe,
And tell the doleful tragedy,
   That late was played at Globe
For no man that can sing and say
But was scared on St Peter's day.
     Oh sorrow, pitiful sorrow, and yet all this is true.

All you that please to understand,
   Come listen to my story,
To see Death with his raking brand
   'Mongst such an auditory;
Regarding neither Cardinal's might,
Nor yet the rugged face of Henry the Eight.
     Oh sorrow, pitiful sorrow, and yet all this is true.

This fearful fire began above,
  A wonder strange and true,
And to the Stage-house did remove,
  As round as tailors clew;
And burnt down both beam and snag,
And did not spare the silken flag.
    Oh sorrow, pitiful sorrow, and yet all this is true.

Out run the knights, out run the lords,
   And there was great ado;
Some lost their hats, and some their swords;
   Then out run Burbage too;
The reprobates, though drunk on Monday,
Prayed for the Fool and Henry Condye.
     Oh sorrow, pitiful sorrow, and yet all this is true.

The perriwigs and drum-heads fry,
   Like to a butter firkin;
A woeful burning did betide
   To many a good buff jerkin.
Then with swollen eyes, like drunken Flemmings,
Distressed stood old stuttering Hemmings,
     Oh sorrow, pitiful sorrow, and yet all this is true.

No shower his rain did there down force
   In all that sunshine weather,
To save that great renowned house;
   Nor thou, O ale-house, neither.
Had it begun below, sans doubt,
The ale-wives would have doused it out.
     Oh sorrow, pitiful sorrow, and yet all this is true.

Be warned, you stage-strutters all,
   Least you again be catched,
And such a burning do befall,
   As to them whose house was thatched;
Forbear your luxury, breeding biles,
And lay up that expense for tiles.
     Oh sorrow, pitiful sorrow, and yet all this is true.

Go draw you a petition
   And do you not abhor it,
And get, with low submission,
   A licence to beg for it
In churches, sans churchwardens checks,
In Surrey and in Middlesex.
     Oh sorrow, pitiful sorrow, and yet all this is true.

11. *Opening Scene from* The Knight of the Burning Pestle *by Beaumont and Fletcher*

(This extract has been slightly edited, with additional stage directions, for modern reading.)

We are in the Blackfriars Playhouse (an indoor theatre) in the year 1613. A play is about to begin, and its title, The London Merchant, *is displaced hung up on a board. Several gentlemen are sitting on stools upon the stage. Among the spectators seated below the stage are a Citizen (a grocer), his Wife, and their apprentice Ralph. The boy actor who is to speak the play's Prologue now enters, advances to the front of the stage, and begins:*

PROLOGUE.   From all that's near the court, from all that's great
              Within the compass of the city walls,
              We now have brought our scene—

(Citizen leaps upon the Stage and interrupts him angrily)

CIT.   Hold your peace, goodman boy!

PROL.   What do you mean, sir?

CIT.   That *you* have no good meaning. In all the seven years there have been plays at this house, I have observed that you have been ever jibing at our citizens and now you call your play *The London Merchant*. Down with your title, boy, down with your title!

PROL.   Are you a member of the noble city?

CIT.   I am.

PROL.   And a freeman?

CIT.   *(Proudly)* Yea, and *(prouder still)* a grocer.

PROL.   So, grocer; then, by your sweet favour, we intend no abuse to the city.

CIT.   No, sir? yes, sir! if you were not resolved to play the jackanapes and to abuse your betters, what need have you for new subjects? Why could you not be contented, as others are, with the legend of Dick Whittington, or the Life and Death of Sir Thomas Gresham, with the building of the Royal Exchange?

PROL.   You seem to be an understanding man; what would you have us do, sir?

CIT.   Why, present something notably in honour of the commons of the city.

PROL.   Why, what do you say to the Life and Death of fat Drake, or the Repairing of Fleet Privies?[1]

CIT.   I do not like that; but I will have a citizen, and he shall be of my own trade.

PROL.   Oh, you should have told us your mind a month since; our play is ready to begin now.

CIT.   (*Doggedly*) 'Tis all one for that; I *will* have a grocer in it, and he shall do admirable things.

PROL.   What will you have him do?

CIT.   Marry, I will have—(*he pauses, momentarily at a loss for ideas*)

WIFE.   (*Eagerly from her place in the audience*) Husband, husband!

RALPH.   (*At her side, trying to keep her quiet*) Peace, mistress!

WIFE.   Hold thy peace, Ralph; I know what I do, I warrant thee.   Husband, husband!

CIT.   What say'st thou, sweetheart?

WIFE.   Let him kill a lion with a Pestle, husband! Let him kill a lion with a Pestle![2]

---

[1] One guesses that fat Drake must have been a well-known London character who had recently died, and that the Fleet Privies were some sort of public lavatories by the Fleet Ditch (near Fleet Street) whose repair, perhaps overdue, had been a subject of gossip. Perhaps fat Drake was the keeper of them.

[2] Keeping it all in the grocery trade.   The pestle and mortar for grinding up sugar, etc., were the grocer's familiar implements.

CIT.   So he shall. (*Turning to the Prologue*) I'll have him kill a lion with a Pestle.

WIFE.   Husband! shall I come up, husband?

CIT.   Ay, sweetheart.—Ralph, help your mistress this way.—Pray gentlemen, make her a little room. I pray you, sir, lend me your hand to help up my wife. I thank, you; so! (*Wife is helped up on to the Stage, with some fuss and commotion. She is not slim*)

WIFE.   By your leave, gentlemen all. (*She arrives at last*) I'm something troublesome. I'm a stranger here; I was ne'er at one of these plays, as they say, before; but I nearly came to see Jane Shore once; and my husband hath promised me, any time this twelvemonth, to take me to the Bold Beauchamps,[1] but in truth he did not. I pray you bear with me.

CIT.   Boy, let my wife and I have a couple of stools, and then begin; and look to it, let the grocer do rare things.

(*Stools are brought, and they sit down*)

PROL.   But, sir, we have never a boy to play him. Every one of us hath a part already.

WIFE.   Husband, husband, for God's sake, let Ralph play him! Beshrew me, if I do not think he will go beyond them all.

CIT.   Well remembered wife.—Come up Ralph! I'll tell you, gentlemen; let but lend him a suit of reparrel[2] and necessaries, and, by gad, if anyone in this house has fault to find with him, I'll be hanged!

(*Ralph comes up onto the Stage*)

WIFE.   (*To the Prologue*) I pray you, youth, let him have a suit of reparrel. (*To those around her*) I'll be sworn, gentlemen, my husband tells you true. He will

---

[1] *Jane Shore* and *The Bold Beauchamps* were two popular plays.
[2] Apparel (The Citizen mispronounces).

act sometimes at our house, so that all the neighbours cry out at him! He will roar up a couraging part so loud in the garret, that we are all so feared, I warrant you, that we tremble. We frighten our children with him; whenever they are unruly, we do but cry, "Ralph comes, Ralph comes!" to them, and they'll be as quiet as lambs. (*Ralph is coy at all this praise*) Hold up thy head, Ralph; show the gentlemen what thou cans't do; speak a huffing part; I warrant you the gentlemen will accept of it.

CIT. Do, Ralph, do.

RALPH. (*Strikes an attitude and begins to give a great performance*)

By heaven, methinks, it were an easy leap
To pluck bright honour from the pale-faced moon,
Or dive into the bottom of the sea,
Where never fathom-line touch'd any ground,
And pluck up drowned honour from the lake of hell....

CIT. How say you, gentlemen? Is it not as I told you?

WIFE. Nay, gentlemen, he hath played before, my husband says, Musidorus,[1] before the wardens of the Grocers' Company.

CIT. Ay, and he should have played Jeronimo[2] with a shoemaker for a wager.

PROL. He shall have a suit of apparel, if he will go into the tiring house.

CIT. In, Ralph! in, Ralph! and do your best for the grocery trade, if thou lovest me.

(*Ralph goes in*)

---

[1] A popular romantic play, author unknown, about "*Mucedorus the King's son of Valentia, and Amadine the King's daughter of Aragon*". It was said to be "very delectable and full of mirth".

[2] "*Jeronimo*" was an alternative popular title for Kyd's "*Spanish Tragedy*" (see Chapter 5).

WIFE. I warrant our Ralph will look finely when he's dress'd.

PROL. But what will you have it called?

CIT. The Grocer's Honour.

PROL. Methinks The Knight of the Burning Pestle were better.

WIFE. I'll be sworn, husband, that's as good a name as can be.

CIT. Let is be so; begin, begin; my wife and I will sit down.

PROL. (*With relief*) I pray you, do.

CIT. What stately music have you? You have shawms?

PROL. Shawms? No.

CIT. No? I'm a thief if my mind did not give me to think you had. Ralph plays a stately part, so we must needs have shawms. I'll pay the cost of them myself, rather than we'll be without them.

PROL. So you may have to do.

CIT. (*Nettled*) Why, and so I will do. There's two shillings; lets have the waits of Southwark! They are rare fellows as any are in England, and that will fetch them o'er the river, with a vengeance, as if they were mad.

PROL. You shall have them. Will you sit down, then?

CIT. Ay.—Come, wife.

WIFE. Sit you merry all, gentlemen; I'm bold to sit amongst you for my ease.

(*They all settle down, and the Prologue is at last able to resume his opening speech*)

PROL. From all that's near the court, from all that's great
Within the compass of the city walls,
We now have brought our scene: Fly far from hence
All private taxes, all immodest phrases;

Whatever doth but seem like vice, fly hence!
For wicked mirth never true pleasure brings,
But honest minds are pleased with honest things
(Having finished his opening, the Prologue turns to go. On his way out he says aside to the Citizen) Thus much for what *we* do; but, for Ralph's part, you must answer for yourself.

CIT.   Take you no care for Ralph; he'll discharge himself, I warrant you.

WIFE.   I' faith, gentlemen, I'll give my word for Ralph.

(The first actors enter . . . and the play begins.)